DATE DUE

NO 1 95			
00 99			
MY 7 02			

DEMCO 38-296

"How did these kids get so good so fast?"

—Allan Wallach, *Newsday*

Good? These writers are much more than that. In this collection of seven plays by writers aged sixteen to eighteen, each writer attempts to go beyond the story of his or her play to reach bold conclusions, full of ideas that reverberate. And each one delivers.

IMAGINE: John Lennon's two greatest fans meet hours before his death.

EBONY: Ebony's mother made mistakes with men, but Ebony is determined not to repeat them.

SPARKS IN THE PARK: Barry's love life is out of control, so he's writing a play to forget. But his characters start to take over . . .

AND THE AIR DIDN'T ANSWER: Does God exist? Dan's wild fantasies help him find an answer.

SENIORITY: Sisters confront each other, and nothing will ever be the same again.

CHILDREN: Jenny's mother, Julia, is more like a friend than a mother. Jenny's *so* lucky. Isn't she?

WOMEN AND WALLACE: Women love Wallace. But *he* can't love *them* until he can come to terms with his mother's death.

Cosmic doubt becomes comic, humor delights and shocks, fantasy blends with reality in this surprising and provocative collection. The voices in these plays are powerful ones, because the Young Playwrights Festival wants to hear what young people have to say. If you're under nineteen, why not write a play and enter? You can't lose.

WENDY LAMB is a consulting editor of books for young readers at Delacorte Press. Her stories and articles have appeared in several magazines, and she edited *Meeting the Winter Bike Rider* (plays from the 1983 and 1984 Young Playwrights Festivals) and *The Ground Zero Club* (plays from the 1985 and 1986 Young Playwrights Festivals), both available in Laurel-Leaf editions.

Praise for
MEETING THE WINTER BIKE RIDER
and Other Prize-winning Plays from the
1983 and 1984 Young Playwrights Festivals

Edited by Wendy Lamb
Introduction by Gerald Chapman

An ALA Best Book for Young Adults

"This collection . . . presents a variety of material which is entertaining to read and easily performed. But more important, this volume should serve as encouragement and inspiration to other talented young people. Statements from each author . . . indicate that gifted individuals, from whatever background, geographic area, or age group, can be appreciated and rewarded."
—*School Library Journal*

"An exciting collection. . . . Topics are varied, sophisticated, and well-developed. While the plays are excellent entertainment, the short essays, introductions, and biographies of the playwrights are fascinating. Their descriptions of what participating in the Young Playwrights Festivals and winning meant to them, and how it affected their lives, are exciting and should inspire other young people to try to participate." —*Voice of Youth Advocates*

and for
THE GROUND ZERO CLUB
**and Other Prize-winning Plays from the
1985 and 1986 Young Playwrights Festivals**

Edited by Wendy Lamb
Introduction by Peggy C. Hansen

"The six plays in this anthology . . . display a wide range of styles and themes yet share a common maturity and sensitivity to the ironies of life. . . . These are multi-faceted plays to be read, discussed, performed, and viewed by young adults and adults alike. Of special interest to students will be the notes by the author which follow each play. Bravo!"

—*School Library Journal* (starred review)

"Rewarding and engaging . . . inspirational for the budding dramatist as well as accessible for recreational reading. . . . This is a must for YA collections."   —*Booklist*

The seven plays in this anthology were selected from those given full productions or staged readings in the Foundation of the Dramatists Guild's Young Playwrights Festival at Playwrights Horizons in New York City. Information on the Young Playwrights Festival is available from the Foundation of the Dramatists Guild, 234 West 44 Street, New York, New York 10036. Phone: (212) 575-7796.

YOUNG PLAYWRIGHTS FESTIVAL STAFF

Nancy Quinn, Producing Director
Sheri M. Goldhirsch, Managing Director
Cynthia S. Stokes, Education Coordinator
Reginald Jackson, Administrative Assistant

YOUNG PLAYWRIGHTS FESTIVAL COMMITTEE

Stephen Sondheim, Chairman
Andre Bishop
Christopher Durang
Ruth Goetz
Micki Grant
Carol Hall

Marsha Norman
Nancy Quinn
Mary Rodgers
Alfred Uhry
Wendy Wasserstein

In 1987 and 1988, major funding for the Young Playwrights Festival was provided by: Barker Welfare Foundation, Charles Ulrick and Josephine Bay Foundation, Chase Manhattan Bank, Eleanor Naylor Dana Charitable Trust, Dramatists Guild Fund, Educational Foundation of America, Ettinger Foundation, Exxon Corporation, Samuel Goldwyn Company, Stephen Graham, George Link Jr. Foundation, MCA Foundation, Metropolitan Life Foundation, New York State Council on the Arts, Rockefeller Foundation, Richard and Dorothy Rodgers Foundation, Shubert Foundation, Wallace Funds. To all of the above and to its many other contributors, the Festival extends grateful appreciation.

From the 1987 and 1988
Young Playwrights Festivals
Produced by
The Foundation of
the Dramatists Guild

SPARKS
IN THE
PARK
and
Other Prize-winning
Plays

EDITED BY
Wendy Lamb
Introduction by Nancy Quinn

Riverside Community College
Library

4800 Magnolia Avenue
JUL   '92   Riverside, California 92506

Published by
Dell Publishing
Bantam Doubleday Dell Publishing Group, Inc.
666 Fifth Avenue
New York, New York 10103

PHOTO CREDITS:
Front cover:
Bellina Logan as Sarah, Josh Hamilton as Wallace, in WOMEN AND WALLACE,
performed at Playwrights Horizons, New York City, September–October 1988.
Copyright © 1988 by Tess Steinkolk

Back cover:
Kevin Corrigan, Copyright © 1988 by Alex Wasinski
Robert Kerr, Copyright © 1988 by Tess Steinkolk
Pamela Mariva Mshana, Copyright © 1987 by Wayne Moore
Debra Terri Neff, Copyright © 1987, by Linda Alaniz, Martha Swope Associates
Jonathan Marc Sherman, Copyright © 1988 by Martha Swope
Noble Mason Smith, Copyright © 1989, by Murat Sinanoglu
Eric Ziegenhagen, Copyright © 1988, by Mary Lynn Kirby

IMAGINE Copyright © 1989 by Kevin Corrigan
AND THE AIR DIDN'T ANSWER Copyright © 1989 by Robert Kerr
EBONY Copyright © 1989 by Pamela Mariva Mshana
CHILDREN Copyright © 1989 by Debra Terri Neff
WOMEN AND WALLACE Copyright © 1989 by Jonathan Marc Sherman
SPARKS IN THE PARK Copyright © 1988, 1989 by Noble Mason Smith
All amateur and professional performing rights for SPARKS IN THE PARK are
controlled by Samuel French, Inc., 45 West 25 Street, New York, N.Y. 10010
SENIORITY Copyright © 1989 by Eric Ziegenhagen

Introduction Copyright © 1989 by Nancy Quinn
Collection Copyright © 1989 Dell Publishing

ISBN: 0-440-20415-1

RL: 5.7

Printed in the United States of America

October 1989

10 9 8 7 6 5 4 3 2 1

KRI

CONTENTS

In memory of
GERALD CHAPMAN
1949–1987
The first artistic director
of the Foundation of the Dramatists Guild
Young Playwrights Festival

INTRODUCTION

So, you want to write a play. What should you write about? To quote Barry from *Sparks in the Park,* "the most important things a writer can write about are those that happen to him . . . really happen." Dorothy in *The Wizard of Oz* says, almost like a prayer, "There's no place like home." Home is a good subject for a play. Home, or school, or the town you live in, or a hobby you love, or a person you know. When you share your world with us, your audience, you change the way we look at our world. How we feel about it will never be quite the same.

Most of the plays in this book started out with an event that really happened to the writer. The others started with an event or series of events that the writers observed, events that affected them in a very personal way.

In *Imagine,* Kevin Corrigan took an event that really happened, the senseless murder of John Lennon. And then, as his title suggests, he imagined two young people meeting for the first time on that day. He took an event that shocked and saddened all of us and showed it to us in a different way. Many of us remember what we were doing when we "heard the news, oh boy" (to quote Lennon himself), and it all comes back to us as we watch these two young people leave to get a pizza.

Jonathan Sherman's mother really did die when he was six years old. In *Women and Wallace,* Jonathan makes that very personal, devastating event have meaning for all of us, and not just because we feel sorry for Wallace. Jonathan has written a tragic comedy (or is it a comic tragedy?) about abandonment and death, about trust and love. We laugh as we watch Wallace grow up, but we also nod sadly because we, too, come to understand that nothing, not even a dead mother, gives us "carte blanche for a lifetime of screwing up."

Robert Kerr's questioning of his religious beliefs really did cost him a summer job. He moves *And the Air Didn't Answer* beyond that event by using fantasy, and it is the juxtaposition of Dan's view of reality with Dan's fantasies that propels the play forward. By the way, be sure to read Bob's notes at the end of his play. As he points out, playwriting is rewriting. When *Air* was in rehearsal for the Preliminary Readings Series, director Christopher Durang decided to have the cast read all of Bob's different versions. *And the Air Didn't Answer,* as produced in the 1988 Young Playwrights Festival, combined elements from all of these versions.

Noble Mason Smith really did receive a copy of the Young Playwrights Festival "Write a Play" poster, and it inspired him to write a play about writing a play. Here, again, the juxtaposition of fantasy and reality points up our friend Barry's lack of awareness (and seeming lack of interest) in the reality that is his life.

While *Ebony, Seniority,* and *Children* are all keen observations of the events of life, and the seeming inevitability of those events, their authors also raise a question that haunts us all: "What's going to happen to me? What will become of me?"

Pamela Mshana's Ebony knows what's *not* going to happen to her. She is not going to have a life like her mother's. She's determined. But her quest for love, for someone to take care of her, lands her in a situation that seems even worse than her mother's.

Jenny in Debra Neff's *Children* has what most young people pray for: a parent who doesn't say "Where were you?" "You're late!" "You're too young," or "No!" But this backfires. Jenny is terrified; she doesn't know what's going to happen—either to her or to her mother.

In Eric Ziegenhagen's *Seniority,* Debbie seems smart and very together. Unlike her sister, Fiona, she's got it all figured out. She's spending the summer in Europe, then going to college, then. . . . She's not worried about what's going to become of her until she's confronted with her inability to talk to guys, to get a date. Suddenly all the careful planning doesn't seem to matter.

Children's books often end "And they all lived happily ever after." The plays in this volume all end with a big question mark. You don't have to have solutions to write a play. In fact, a good play always makes us wonder.

So, how did we pick these plays? What will happen to your play if you send it to us? (And we certainly hope that you will.)

The Foundation of the Dramatists Guild started the Young Playwrights Festival in 1982 to provide young playwrights the opportunity of working on their plays with the theater's top professionals. Since then we have given professional productions or staged readings to fifty-two plays by forty-nine writers aged eight to eighteen. So far, forty-three of our playwrights have continued to write plays and to work in the professional theater.

Every spring we send about fifty thousand information posters to schools, clubs, drama groups, summer camps, and individuals. There are very few rules: you must be no older than eighteen and the play must be an original (no adaptations). You can submit more than one play, and collaborations are fine as long as all of your fellow collaborators are also no older than eighteen.

Your play will be evaluated by a theater professional—an actor, director, or playwright—and we'll send you a copy of the evaluation. Many writers say they send us their plays because they want the feedback. In fact, Jonathan Sherman says he started sending us his plays because he didn't believe his family and teachers, who kept telling him how talented he was. He wanted the unvarnished truth about his writing. We disappointed him by agreeing with his fan club.

Each year about twenty-five plays are recommended to the Young Playwrights Festival Committee, whose members in 1987 and 1988 were Andre Bishop, Christopher Durang, Jules Feiffer, Ruth Goetz, Micki Grant, A. R. Gurney, Jr., Carol Hall, Murray Horwitz, Marsha Norman, Mary Rodgers, Stephen Sondheim, Alfred Uhry, and Wendy Wasserstein. The Committee reads these plays and selects ten to fifteen of them for the YPF Preliminary Readings Series. We bring these playwrights to New York City, where each of their plays is given a staged reading with a professional director, dramaturg, and cast. The YPF Committee attends the readings, meets with the playwrights, and then selects the plays to be fully produced (usually, an evening's worth—that is, as many plays as can be presented in two and a half or three hours) and to receive professionally staged readings. These are always tough decisions to make. All of your plays deserve our time and attention and further work.

If you want to know more about playwriting, call us or write to us. That's what we're here for, to encourage and assist young writers, and besides, we enjoy hearing from you. Our address and phone number are on page vii.

There are now about ten regional young playwrights groups that we helped to start. One may be near you. These groups offer classes or workshops in playwriting skills, some taught by professional playwrights. Some groups also have competitions and present the plays of their young writers.

So, look at the world around you. Write a play about your world, your feelings, your dreams. Read plays. See plays. Send us your plays. Just think—*your* work could be in the next volume of plays from the Young Playwrights Festival.

Nancy Quinn
Producing Director
Young Playwrights Festival

IMAGINE
A Play in One Act

by Kevin Corrigan
(age eighteen when play was written)
Bronx, New York

NOTE:
For the purpose of publication in this collection, certain words
have been changed by the playwright, and some profanity has been
deleted from the working script of the play as performed at Playwrights Horizons, New York City, May 6, 1988.

Imagine was performed in a reading at Playwrights Horizons on May 6, 1988, directed by Clinton Turner Davis. John Patrick Shanley was the playwright adviser. The cast:

JOE . . . . JACE ALEXANDER
KATHY . . . . LAUREN TOM

SETTING: 72nd Street and Central Park West, New York City, across from the Dakota, an apartment house.

TIME: Monday, December 8, 1980, around 6:00 P.M.

Lights up on JOE, *seventeen, sitting on a park bench. He holds a copy of John Lennon's new album,* Double Fantasy, *and beside him sits a radio, playing music. He sports a pair of "Lennon" spectacles, a Lennonesque hat and scarf, and a denim jacket covered with Beatle buttons. He seems restless and anxious. He is hawking the Dakota's main gate in the hopes of spotting his hero. After a minute he thinks he sees John and leaps up. He gets as far as the curb before realizing it isn't him. Frustrated, he returns to the bench. He checks his watch and scans the darkening Manhattan sky.*

Just then, KATHY, *an attractive blonde, also seventeen, enters from stage left.* JOE *watches as she passes by the bench and over to the curb. Wearing many of the same buttons as* JOE *and carrying a copy of the* Revolver *LP,* KATHY *also passes for a Beatlemaniac.*

The two kids become shy and self-conscious. They are deeply interested in one another but can hardly bring themselves to do anything about it. With this, a little game ensues: KATHY *glances at* JOE, *and he looks away, then he glances at her and she looks away. Both become excited.*

KATHY: Excuse me, do you have the time?

(JOE *turns down the volume on his radio and checks.*)

JOE: It's ten to six.

KATHY: Thank you.

(JOE *once again thinks he sees John. He darts wildly toward the street, startling* KATHY. *Stops dead at the curb, coming to the same realization as before. Again frustrated, he puts his radio down on the sidewalk, looks at the traffic, and mumbles to himself.*)

KATHY: Excuse me, but where did you get that button?

JOE: Which one?

KATHY *(pointing):* That one.

JOE: This one? Oh, this one I got at an auction down at the Sheraton Plaza. You know that Beatles convention they have every year?

KATHY: Yeah, I went to one in Baltimore.

JOE: Did you?

KATHY: Yeah.

JOE: That's cool. Well, I got this one at the convention they had just last month at the Sheraton Plaza. Paid ninety-six dollars for it.

KATHY: Wow!

JOE: Yeah, it's rare. *(Beat.)*

KATHY: Do you like the Beatles?

JOE: Yeah . . . *(kidding)* just a little. *(They laugh.)*

KATHY: I like them, too.

JOE: Yeah, they're the greatest.

KATHY: They are. The greatest!

JOE: Yeah, I agree.

KATHY: Who's your favorite? Beatle, I mean.

JOE: I'd have to say John. John's my favorite.

KATHY: Really?

JOE: Yeah. I idolize him, as a matter of fact. He's just, uh . . . really the greatest thing that's ever happened to me. Greatest person, I mean, to come into my life. I love him. Who's your favorite?

KATHY: For me, it's a tie between John and Paul.

JOE: A tie? There's no contest.

KATHY: You don't like Paul?

JOE: He's all right, but . . .

KATHY: But what?

JOE: I mean, he's cool—he was one of the Beatles, right? But . . . he's got this attitude I just don't care for.

KATHY: What attitude?

JOE: He's a homeboy.

KATHY: He is not!

JOE: Yes, he is. He's a homeboy. A stuck-up homeboy.

KATHY: I don't think so. I think he's cute.

JOE: Well, all girls do. *(He goes back to the bench.)*

KATHY: Are you waiting for John Lennon?

JOE: Yeah, I want him to sign my album.

KATHY: Which one? *(He holds it up.)* Oh, *Double Fantasy!*

JOE: Yeah, I just bought it yesterday. What album do you have there? *(She holds it up.)* *Revolver!* That's a great album.

KATHY: Yeah, it's my favorite.

JOE: Yeah. You know what my favorite song on that album is? *(He motions for her to come over to the bench.)* This one here. "Tomorrow Never Knows." I love that song! *(Sings first line.)* John wrote that, you know. Just goes to show what a genius he is. You gonna try to get him to sign this?

KATHY: Yeah. How did you find out he lives here?

JOE: I read it in *Rolling Stone* magazine. There was a picture of him and everything in front of the entranceway over there. It said, "John Lennon in front of the Dakota on West Seventy-second Street." One time I came down here, I think it was about a year ago, and I saw him.

KATHY: Really?

JOE: Yep. Swear to God. No lie. I saw him walkin' through the park with his son, Sean. I was really excited when I saw him, too, 'cause I never seen a famous person before—much less my idol! I yelled out, "Hey, John!" and he turned around to look, and I waved, and he waved back.

KATHY: Wow!

JOE: Yeah. I tell ya, that was probably the greatest moment of my life. I hope he gets back before it gets really dark. I hate being downtown late.

KATHY: Where did he go?

JOE: He went to a recording session or something. That's what the guard told me. He wouldn't tell me where the studio was, though. Those guys never tell you stuff like that.

KATHY: How long ago did he leave?

JOE: Well, when I asked the guard, it was around five o'clock, and he said John had just left with Yoko.

(KATHY, *a little disappointed, gets back up and goes to the curb.*)

KATHY: He probably won't be back for hours, then.

JOE: Yeah, that's what I'm afraid of. *(Pause.)* I was really pissed off, too, you know? 'Cause I got here around three-thirty, right? Then I waited for about an hour, and then I got a little hungry, so I went to get something to eat. What happens? By the time I got back, he'd already come and gone. *(A beat as he removes his scarf.)* Kind of warm out for December, isn't it?

(KATHY nods, then slowly starts to exit stage left.)

JOE: What's your name?

(KATHY stops, turns around.)

KATHY: Kathy. *(beat.)* What's yours?

JOE: Paul.

KATHY: Is it, really?

JOE: No. It's Joe.

KATHY: Hi, Joe.

JOE: Oh . . . *(He gets up and shakes her hand.)* Hi, Kathy. Pleased to meet you. My middle name is Paul. It is. I'm gonna change it to John, though.

KATHY: Why don't you change it to Ono?

JOE: Ono? Why would I wanna do that?

KATHY: That's what John changed his middle name to.

(JOE is silent for a moment. He should've known this.)

JOE: I'll think about it.

KATHY: And before he changed it to that, it was Winston.

JOE: So you know a lot about him, then, huh?

KATHY: Pretty much.

JOE: What's his birthday?

KATHY: October 9, 1940.

JOE: Where was he born?

KATHY: Liverpool!

JOE: Okay, wait. Those are easy. What's his mother's name?

KATHY: Julia.

JOE: And where does she live today?

KATHY: She's dead.

JOE: Cause of death?

KATHY: She was hit by a car driven by an off-duty policeman who'd been drinking on July 15, 1958.

JOE: That's pretty good. But I bet I know more.

KATHY: Oh yeah? What was the name of the original drummer of the Beatles?

JOE: Pete Best.

KATHY: Who was their first manager?

JOE: Alan Williams.

KATHY: How many wives did Brian Epstein have?

JOE: He didn't have any. He was a homo!

KATHY: What's George Harrison's favorite food?

JOE: Jelly beans! Actually, they're not his favorite food at all. He just said he liked them. How tall is Ringo Starr?

KATHY: Five feet, eight inches. What's his real name?

JOE: Richard Starkey! Everyone knows that!

KATHY: What kind of toothpaste does he use? (JOE *doesn't answer.*) Ha! I've got you.

JOE: I don't know. What kind of toothpaste does he use?

KATHY: How should I know? *(Beat.)*

JOE: Can you do John's voice?

KATHY: No. Can you?

(He jumps up onto the bench and performs.)

JOE: Are you kidding? *(As Lennon)* "What worries me is that some day a looney will come up, and God knows what will happen then. Once, when we were in Texas during an American tour, several shots were fired at our plane while it was parked on the tarmac. Maybe it was just jealous boyfriends or something, but you never know in America. They're always running around with guns like a lot of cowboys. They think guns are extensions of their arms."

KATHY: That's really good. Where'd you get that from?

JOE: I taped it off the radio. They broadcast this series of old interviews the other night, and I just keep listening to it. I know the whole thing word for word, practically.

KATHY: You know, I met John in England once.

JOE: Get outta here! Did you?

KATHY: Yeah, it was about ten years ago, when I was still living there. I was only about seven or eight, but I can still remember it. My parents had taken me to an exhibition at the London Arts Gallery, and there were a bunch of John's lithographs on display. He happened to be lurking around in the back, and I can remember thinking how much he reminded me of Jesus because he had his beard and mustache, and his hair was down to his shoulders. I went over to him and tugged on his coat. He had on this bright

white dress jacket, and I asked him, "Do you know you look jus'
like Jesus?" and he said, "I've heard that one before," or some'
thing like that, I forget. Anyway, I didn't realize who it was unti'
my mother came over to get me. She went completely crazy. Then'
right before we left, he gave me his autograph on the back of a
postcard with one of his sketches on it.

JOE: That's incredible! That's amazing! You must be stunned!

KATHY: Well, it happened ten years ago.

JOE: Yeah, but still! If that happened to me, I'd be in shock to thi'
very day.

KATHY: It was right after that that I started getting into the
Beatles.

JOE: Yeah, I got into them at a young age myself. *(Beat.)* So yo'
lived in England, huh?

KATHY: Yeah.

JOE: That's the Beatles' homeland!

KATHY: Yeah.

JOE: That's great. *(Beat.)*

KATHY: Could you give me the time again?

JOE: Yeah, it's almost six. Oh, man!

KATHY: What?

JOE: I had a dentist's appointment today at four-thirty and
missed it!

KATHY: Are you sure?

JOE: Well, no. Wait. Is today December eighth or ninth?

KATHY: It's the eighth.

JOE: Oh, it is the eighth? Oh, good. Great. It's tomorrow, then. Had myself worried for a second.

KATHY: What's wrong with your teeth?

JOE: Nothing really. Just gotta go in for a checkup.

KATHY: I might have to get braces.

JOE: Really? Why?

KATHY: This one here.

(She points at the tooth in question, and JOE takes a closer look. He removes his glasses and draws very near to her. Just when it looks like they are about to kiss:)

JOE: Oh, yeah. But that's nothing! I can barely notice it.

KATHY: Really?

JOE: Yeah. Your teeth are really beautiful. *(Beat.)* So you lived in England, huh?

KATHY: The Beatles' homeland.

JOE: Yeah! God, I can't get over that story. So you don't live there anymore? Where do you live now?

KATHY: Down in the Village with my father.

JOE: Oh, just your father? Your parents divorced?

KATHY: No. No, my mother's dead.

JOE: Oh. Sorry to hear that.

KATHY: That's why we moved here. Where do you live?

JOE: Up in the Bronx.

KATHY: Oh. *(Beat.)* Are your parents divorced?

JOE: Yeah. They got divorced when I was four. Grew up with a stepfather and all that. *(Beat.)* So, wudja take the train up here, or somethin'?

KATHY: No, I walked.

JOE: You walked? All the way from the Village?

KATHY: Yeah, I've done it lots of times.

JOE: Don't your legs start to hurt after a while?

KATHY: Not when you've done it as many times as I have.

JOE: Good exercise, anyway. Maybe I should try it.

(KATHY *starts playing with the radio.*)

KATHY: How much longer are you going to wait?

JOE: I don't know. It seems like I've waited long enough.

KATHY: If he went to the studio like that guy said, chances are he'll be there all night. *(She presses the PLAY button, and the song "Imagine" comes on.)*

JOE: Yeah. It's just that I pictured the way everything was gonna happen, ya know? I mean, ya know what I was gonna do? I was gonna go right over to the gate, right as he was coming out, then in a real friendly tone I was gonna say, "Hey, John! How are ya, buddy? You're lookin' real hip today, man! Can you sign my album? It'd be worth a million dollars to me. You're my favorite person in the whole world, ya know." Then he'd say, *(As Lennon)* "Thanks a lot, kid. You're my favorite fan." Then he'd sign the album, hand it back, then he'd invite me into his limousine to wherever he was going. Me and John!

KATHY: That's some imagination you've got.

JOE: I knew you were gonna say that.

(They listen to "Imagine" for the next few moments, sometimes singing along, sometimes looking at each other.)

KATHY: You know, we could come back tomorrow and try again.

JOE *(surprised):* You wanna meet me? *(correcting his tone)* I mean, you wanna meet me here around four or four-thirty?

KATHY: What about your dentist appointment?

JOE *("no problem"):* Who cares about that? (KATHY *laughs.*) I mean, this is important! Right?

KATHY: Yeah! Okay, so we'll meet here at four.

JOE: Okay. *(Beat.)* You know—this is gonna sound stupid—but I'm really glad I met you for some reason. I don't know why.

KATHY: The feeling's mutual.

(They both smile excitedly.)

JOE: Look, are you thirsty? I mean, do you feel like getting a soda or something?

KATHY: Sure.

JOE: Great. It'll be my treat. Are you hungry? We could get some pizza, too, if you want.

KATHY: Do you have that much money on you?

JOE: Yeah, don't worry. I'm loaded this week.

KATHY: Okay.

JOE: Great. Lemme just check something first.

(He stands up and searches his pockets. Pulls out some cash. As he counts it:)

JOE: So, what are some of your favorite Beatles songs, Kathy?

KATHY: Oh, God, there are so many. "Eleanor Rigby," "Let It Be," "The Long and Winding Road."

(They slowly exit stage left, but JOE *has left his copy of* Double Fantasy *on the bench.)*

JOE: All McCartney songs! I don't believe it! What about "Norwegian Wood"? What about "Lucy in the Sky with Diamonds"? What about "Revolution"? All these great John Lennon songs? I've got to educate you. *(He suddenly stops.)* Wait a minute. Where's my album? *(He runs back onstage and picks up the album. He is about to reexit when he is halted by the sight of the Dakota. He looks at it longingly.)*

KATHY: What's the matter?

JOE: I really feel like staying.

(KATHY reenters and stands next to JOE.)

KATHY: Why? You'll be here forever.

JOE: I know, it's just . . . I feel like I should wait. I mean, I really feel like I should wait. I mean, that guy over there's been waiting even longer than I have.

KATHY *(leaning close to him):* What guy?

JOE: That guy. The chubby guy in the dark clothes. With the glasses and the hat. See him?

KATHY: Yeah.

JOE: Yeah, he's been here all day! Strange guy. I was talking with him for a little while before. But he came all the way from Hawaii!

KATHY: Well, there, you see? That's probably why he's waiting so long. He's probably going home tomorrow. Come on. You already live here. You can come down anytime you want. Don't worry, John will still be here tomorrow. I doubt he's going anywhere. *(Beat.)*

JOE *(to himself almost):* Yeah, he'll be here. He'll be here tomorrow. You're right, we can always catch him tomorrow. *(They exit.)*

(Lights slowly fade with "Imagine" playing in the background.)

KEVIN CORRIGAN

For me, life really began in a seventh-grade composition class. Things were such a drag before that class came along. I still hated school, but now there was at least something to look forward to, something I was good at. I'd always been able to draw and paint, but writing seemed more boundless. I was extremely motivated to write.

Playwriting wasn't something I thought about for another five years, and until that time short-story writing was my forte, Edgar Allan Poe being my number-one influence.

Similar to the way I'd chosen writing over painting and drawing, one day I decided to give up writing and try acting. Two years of acting school went by before I decided to adapt my old talent to this new world of theater. I started out by writing simple five-minute scenes, several of which became the stuff of *Delores Was Always Faster,* my first attempt at a play.

With a lot of help and encouragement, *Delores* became a full-length play called *The Boiler Room,* and it was sometime during the development of it that I took time out to write *Imagine.*

I submitted both plays to the Young Playwrights Festival in September 1987, and to my utter astonishment, both were accepted as semifinalists the following spring! *Boiler Room* went on to be a September 1988 finalist, but it's *Imagine* that's been selected for publication, due, I suppose, to its more discreet nature and shorter length.

For the record, *Imagine* was first presented by the Lee Strasberg Theatre Institute in August 1987. It was directed by Richard Perez and featured myself and actress Sara Pearl in the roles of Joe and Kathy.

Looking back, I guess *Imagine* was meant as an expression of my endless love and appreciation for the Beatles. Personally, I like to count it as a tribute to John Lennon. He's the first person I ever idolized. Just by being himself he's inspired me tremendously, in every aspect of my life.

AND THE AIR DIDN'T ANSWER
A Play in One Act

by Robert Kerr
(age seventeen when play was written)
Stillwater, Minnesota

NOTE:
For the purpose of publication in this collection, certain words
have been changed by the playwright from the working script of
the play as performed at Playwrights Horizons, New York City,
September 13 through October 8, 1988.

And the Air Didn't Answer was first performed at Playwrights Horizons on September 13, 1988. The play was directed by Christopher Durang. Morgan Jenness was the playwright adviser. The cast:

DAN WILSON	Robert Sean Leonard
JENNIFER	Jill Tasker
MOTHER	Debra Monk
RENEE	Erica Gimpel
FATHER MCLAUGHLIN, TEACHER, GOD, SCOUT INTERVIEWER	Richard Council
YOUNG BOY, CRUSADER, ABRAHAM, PRODUCER, DANTE, DRUNK IN PARK . .	Jihmi Kennedy
CRUSADER, ISAAC, SALESMAN, ALEX TREBEK, VIRGIL, DRUNK IN PARK	John Augustine

Lights come up on DAN *and* JENNIFER. DAN *is standing behind a pulpit,* JENNIFER *is sitting on a chair in front of him.* DAN *is giving a speech, and* JENNIFER *is listening to him.*

DAN: Just as Peter was the rock upon which our Church was built, faith must be the rock upon which we build our belief. Indeed, faith is the cornerstone upon which the entire Church rests. Faith, we are told, can move mountains. However, faith itself is a mountain. A mountain from which we can draw strength in times of joy . . . and in times of need.

JENNIFER: Bravo! Wonderful speech, Dan!

DAN: Oh, Jennifer. You're just saying that because you're my girlfriend and you're supposed to say things like that.

JENNIFER: No, I mean it. Speaking as the president of the church's youth group, I say it's the best speech we've come up with in a long time. (DAN *and* JENNIFER *hug.*) Just one thing, Dan. Your heart didn't seem to be in it. You may be just practicing right now, but try to sound a little more sincere when you give it Sunday at mass, okay?

DAN: I'm just tired, Jennifer. That's all.

JENNIFER: I don't think so, Dan. I've known you long enough to be able to recognize that look you get when you say something you don't mean.

DAN: What look is that?

JENNIFER: The same one you gave me when I bought you that hideous green sweater for your birthday.

DAN: Hey, I use that sweater once in a while . . . when I have to buff my car.

JENNIFER: Dan!

DAN: Just kidding.

JENNIFER: Seriously, now. What's wrong?

DAN: I don't know what *faith* means anymore.

JENNIFER: Come again?

DAN: I don't know. I just think a lot, and I start to wonder, why does there have to be a God, anyway? Couldn't things be the way they are without some divine power? So I start thinking . . .

JENNIFER: Then you think too much.

DAN: I can't help it, Jen. It isn't that I don't *want* to believe—I really want something to believe in—but I just need a good reason to believe. How do you stay faithful?

JENNIFER: Every time I start to think there isn't a God, I think about something else . . . some assignment from school, some blouse I want to buy at Dayton's . . . sometimes I even think about you. (*Smiles sweetly.*)

DAN: In any case, I don't think I should give this speech on Sunday. It wouldn't feel right to say I feel one way when I really feel another.

JENNIFER: Dan, please. I don't know if I can find anyone else by then. Maybe giving the speech would help bring back your faith. Or maybe you should bring it up in confession with Father McLaughlin. (*Looks at watch.*) I have to go to choir practice now. See you later. (*They kiss, and* JENNIFER *exits.*)

(*Scene shifts to a confessional, where* FATHER MCLAUGHLIN *sits.* DAN *crosses himself and kneels beside him.*)

DAN: Bless me, Father, for I have sinned.

FATHER: Speak your piece, my child.

DAN: Lately I have been losing my faith, Father.

FATHER: *(Sighs.)* It always saddens me to hear that yet another lamb has strayed from the flock. Often, the lamb is a young person, asking for proof of God's existence. But God demands faith, and faith requires discipline. I look at the congregation during Sunday mass, and I see the ills lack of discipline has wrought. *(Several small* BOYS *enter, running around, playing tag, and squealing with delight.)* Parents need to learn that discipline must begin early, even before the children realize how much God loves them. *(One of the* BOYS *starts to pull on* DAN's *sleeve.)* But instead, the children are free to run in the aisles . . .

(In the following section, FATHER MCLAUGHLIN's *speech must continue as smoothly as possible, leaving just enough time in between lines to allow* DAN *and the* BOYS *to say their lines. The flow of the dialogue must continue as smoothly as possible without overlapping speech.)*

BOY: C'mon, Danny, race ya to the back pew.

FATHER: . . . and play their childish games . . .

DAN: Not now! Father McLaughlin's talking.

FATHER: . . . and they never learn the discipline . . .

BOY: So what? Who cares what he says?

FATHER: . . . they need to maintain their faith.

DAN: Well, my ma says I gotta sit still and listen.

FATHER: Then they grow older . . .

BOY: Aw, you're such a mama's boy!

FATHER: . . . and the rebellious adolescent spirit takes over, unchecked . . .

DAN: But it's *mass!* Ma says you're supposed to . . .

FATHER: . . . so these young people decide that Sundays . . .

MOTHER: Dan, be quiet.

DAN: Sorry, Mom.

FATHER: . . . they would rather go fishing or see movies, or whatever it is young people do these days . . .

MOTHER: Just sit still, all right?

FATHER: . . . and they stop coming to church. All because the parents were unwilling to take a stand.

(Pause)

DAN: Father?

FATHER: Yes, my child?

DAN: How may I atone?

FATHER: It is clear that repeating the Hail Mary any number of times will not help you. No, you must learn self-discipline, since it is obvious that your parents either did not know enough or care enough to impose it on you earlier. You shall fast for a day, and forgo sleep for a night. Once you have mastered your body, you will perhaps learn to believe, and then you shall retain your faith. If this atonement seems unusually harsh, I would like you to keep in mind that I was compelled to do the same thing in my days at the seminary when my faith wavered. It helped me, and I expect it will help you. You may go.

(DAN crosses himself and walks to his room, on another part of the stage. MOTHER enters.)

MOTHER: Dan, aren't you coming down to eat?

DAN: I'm not hungry, Mom.

MOTHER: Are you sure? *(She feels* DAN's *forehead.)* Are you feeling well?

DAN: Yeah.

MOTHER: Then why don't you want to eat?

DAN: It's an assignment for health.

MOTHER *(skeptically):* Health?

DAN: Health class. In school. We're supposed to fas . . . er, not eat for a day, and report how we feel.

MOTHER: *(Pause; she still isn't totally convinced.)* This is a *health* class? What kind of teacher tells his students to not eat? It sounds decidedly *un*healthy to me. I'll have to talk with your principal about this. *(Pause.)* Oh, Dan, how are you coming on that application?

DAN: You mean for that job at Scout camp?

MOTHER: Yes. Don't you have to get that in soon?

DAN: I'm going to finish it tonight and I'll have it in the mail tomorrow.

MOTHER: Just be sure to get it in. *(Pause.)* Are you set to give your speech on Sunday?

DAN: I don't know if I'm giving one.

MOTHER: Dan, why not? You always write such fine speeches.

DAN: I couldn't come up with anything to say.

MOTHER: But what will people think? You give a speech every month at mass.

DAN: I've been really busy lately.

MOTHER: Will you do one next month?

DAN: We'll see.

(*A school bell rings.* DAN *moves the kneeler in front of him so that it suggests a school desk.* A FRIEND *enters.*)

FRIEND: Dan! You look like crap! What happened?

DAN (*mumbling unintelligibly*): I didn't get any sleep last night.

FRIEND: What was that?

DAN (*louder and clearer*): I didn't get any sleep last night.

(*A* TEACHER *enters, and Dan's* FRIEND *exits.* DAN *begins to fall asleep during the following.*)

TEACHER: Listen up, class. Today we're going to talk about the Crusades. In 1059, at the Council of Clermont, Pope Urban II called upon the Christian kings of Europe to levy armies . . .

(DAN *is now asleep. Lights change, and two* CRUSADERS *enter, wearing leather jackets, and one carries a length of pipe. The one with the pipe taps* DAN *on the shoulder, startling him awake.*)

FIRST CRUSADER: Hey, you! (*Pause.*) You! I'm talking to ya! (DAN *looks up at him.*) Lord's Prayer!

DAN: Huh?

CRUSADER: Lord's Prayer! Say it!

DAN: Our Father, who art in heaven, hallowed be thy name. Thy kingdom come . . .

CRUSADER: Enough. You know it.

DAN: Who are you?

CRUSADER: We's the Crusaders.

DAN: The who?

CRUSADER: The Crusaders. We does Crusades . . . ya know, holy wars. We look around for dudes who ain't in the right gang, the *Christian* gang. If they can't say the Lord's Prayer, we know they ain't in the right gang. So we "converts" 'em. *(Slaps pipe in his hand. The other* CRUSADER *laughs idiotically.)*

DAN: Why?

CRUSADER: Cuz we's on a mission from God! Right now, we're on our way over to Forty-second and Grand, cuz, ya see, the Moslem gang done moved in on our turf, and we don't like heathens on our turf, ya see, so we're gonna bust some heads . . . (SECOND CRUSADER *laughs.* FIRST CRUSADER *sees someone offstage.)* Hey, you! In the skullcap! Lord's Prayer! *(Pause.)* Well, suppose we just teach it to you, then. (SECOND CRUSADER *laughs, and both* CRU-SADERS *exit.)*

TEACHER *(waking* DAN *up):* Dan. Oh, Da-an. Have pleasant dreams? How about if you catch up on your sleep after class. In detention, perhaps? (TEACHER *moves the kneeler so that it is now beside* DAN, *like a table in detention. The* TEACHER *then motions for* RENEE *to enter. She pulls up a chair and sits next to the kneeler, across from* DAN.)

RENEE: Is this school a prison, or is the principal this uptight only for today? I mean, I was halfway to school when I remembered I had to send in my dues for Greenpeace, so I went home, got the envelope, dropped it off at the post office, and then came to school. I missed first hour, which is study hall anyway, and they sent me up here, to *detention*.

DAN: You missed the first forty-five minutes of school because you had to mail a letter?

RENEE: That's the sort of thing that happens when you bike to school.

DAN: Don't you have a car?

RENEE: Never drive 'em. The air's polluted enough already.

TEACHER: Quiet over there. One person to a table.

(RENEE *starts to leave and then turns back to* DAN.)

RENEE: Oh, by the way, my name's Renee. I'm new here.

DAN: I'm Dan.

TEACHER: I'm talking to *you,* young lady.

RENEE: Peace. *(She exits.)*

(Scene changes to church where DAN *rehearsed his speech earlier.* JENNIFER *is waiting for* DAN *when he enters.)*

JENNIFER: You're a half hour late! Where were you?

DAN: Detention.

JENNIFER: Detention? That's a first for you. How come?

DAN: It's a long story.

JENNIFER: Oh, well. There's this girl in first-period study hall— maybe you saw her in detention—some hippie kook named Renee something-or-other. Anyway, she walks in right at the end of first period, and she said it was because she had to send something to one of those hippie organizations—Green Peas, or something. So she got detention. (DAN *doesn't react.*) Are you set to practice your speech again?

DAN: I'm not going to give it.

JENNIFER: Why not?

DAN: I don't feel all that faithful.

JENNIFER: Did you talk to Father McLaughlin?

DAN: Yes, and as a result I'm tired and hungry and I don't have one bit of faith.

JENNIFER *(handing him a Bible):* Here, why don't you try reading something from the Bible? Maybe that will remind you how loving God is.

DAN: All right. (DAN *opens the Bible and starts to read. The lights fade a little on him as the following scene takes place on another part of the stage. As he reads, the biblical* ABRAHAM *and* ISAAC *appear onstage.)*

GOD'S VOICE: Abraham! (ABRAHAM *doesn't notice.)* Hey, Abraham! *(Hearing the voice for the first time,* ABRAHAM *looks around fearfully.)* On your knees! (ABRAHAM *kneels.)*

ABRAHAM: Yes, Heavenly Father.

GOD'S VOICE: Would you do *anything* for me?

ABRAHAM: Of course, Heavenly Father.

GOD'S VOICE: If I asked you to, would you climb to the top of Mount Sinai and scream at the top of your lungs, "I'm an effeminate moron!"

ABRAHAM: Yes, and I would even add, "I'm proud of it!"

GOD'S VOICE: Would you eat earthworms fried in the fat of a leprous ass?

ABRAHAM: Gladly, and I wouldn't even add ketchup.

(GOD *enters.)*

GOD: All right, then. What I want you to do is this—go up into the mountains and make a sacrifice.

ABRAHAM: Is that all? I do that all the time.

GOD: This time you must sacrifice your son, Isaac.

(ISAAC *squeals in terror and clutches* ABRAHAM's *leg.*)

ABRAHAM: Isaac? If I kill him, who will clean up the camels' dung? Why Isaac?

GOD: I get tired of seeing those cute little lambs dying all the time.

ABRAHAM: But he's my own son!

GOD: Are you turning chicken on me? (*A child's taunting song.*) Abraham's a chicken! Abraham's a chicken!

ABRAHAM: All right. I'll do it.

(*During the following speech* ABRAHAM *performs each action as* GOD *tells him to.*)

GOD: Great! Now build an altar with those stones . . . nice and high . . . just like that. Next, make a fire, a big one . . . there's nothing I like better than a big fire, except a big flood, of course. Okay, tie down Isaac . . . there you go, good and tight, so he can't get away. . . . (ISAAC *whimpers and writhes in fear.*) Ooooh, look at him squirm! (GOD *hands* ABRAHAM *a knife.*) Raise up this knife. Really high, now. . . . When I count to three, drive it right into his chest . . . one . . . two . . . two and a half . . . two and three quarters. . . . Wow, you really did mean it! All right, let him go.

ABRAHAM: What?

GOD: Let him go. I changed my mind. There's a ram caught in that bush over there. Kill that instead. I'm hungry for lamb chops anyway.

ABRAHAM: But didn't you want me to sacrifice Isaac to prove my faith?

ISAAC: Shhhh!

GOD: Hey, I was just kidding. (ABRAHAM *pouts.*) Come on, don't pout like that. You didn't take me seriously, did you? For heaven's sake, some people just can't take a joke!

(ABRAHAM, ISAAC, *and* GOD *exit.* DAN *is closing the Bible.*)

JENNIFER: Well? Did it help?

DAN: No.

JENNIFER: Not at all?

DAN: I'm sorry, Jennifer. I just read the story of Isaac and Abraham, and it seems to me that only a cruel God would tell someone to sacrifice his own son.

JENNIFER: You aren't getting the point, Dan. The story doesn't show God's cruelty, it shows his mercy.

DAN: Mercy? If I took hostages at gunpoint, held them for a few hours, and finally changed my mind and let them go, I'd be arrested for kidnapping, not mercy.

JENNIFER: It just isn't the same thing, Dan. Can't you see? Why don't you just put your faith in God? Like you said in your speech, faith can move mountains.

DAN: I've tried to have faith, to just believe, but I just can't do it. I need some kind of proof. If faith means putting aside my own judgment, I'd rather leave mountains alone.

JENNIFER: Obviously you haven't been trying hard enough. I admit it isn't easy, but you've got to work at faith all the time.

DAN: I'm just not the kind of person who can do that. I need to question, I need to know for sure. Faith is just not enough anymore.

JENNIFER: Are you saying you don't believe in God?

DAN: I don't know what I believe right now. I suppose there could be some kind of higher being, but I can't find it in the Bible or in church. In fact, I feel really uncomfortable in church lately. It seems to be a place for the faithful, and I feel out of place.

JENNIFER: Does this mean you won't be coming to mass anymore? What about the retreat a week from Friday?

DAN: If I quit coming to mass, it kind of rules out doing anything with the youth group.

JENNIFER: If you're quitting the youth group, when will we ever see each other?

DAN: We can go to movies. Prom's coming up. . . .

JENNIFER: I'm president of the youth group. That takes up a lot of time.

DAN: It doesn't take up all your time.

JENNIFER: Still, it just wouldn't be the same anymore.

DAN: That doesn't mean we can't go out, does it?

(*A pause while* DAN *and* JENNIFER *look at each other. Then* JENNIFER *picks up the lectern and exits. Blackout. After a pause, lights come up on* DAN *and* RENEE *in the woods.*)

DAN: I still say you could have ordered a salad instead.

RENEE: I just think it's immoral to buy food from a place that kills to feed its customers.

DAN: Renee, we're talking about Mr. Steak, not Sweeney Todd.

RENEE: I'm still not going to give my money to a restaurant that—

DAN: It was *my* money. I was going to pay for dinner.

RENEE: And I won't give them your money, either.

DAN: Then why didn't you tell me you were a vegetarian before I made the reservations? *(Pause.)* Listen, I'm sorry. I'm just crabby because I'm hungry. Here, give me a hug. *(They hug.)*

RENEE: I'm sorry, too. Look, there's a good spot to sit down. *(Points to a spot beside the bushes. They sit there.)*

DAN: Okay, so now what?

RENEE: Just sit here and feel the life around you. *(Pause. RENEE breathes deeply and starts to meditate. After a few moments she suddenly breaks this reverie.)* By the way, did you break up with that Jennifer last month?

DAN: Yes.

RENEE: Why?

DAN: Well, she's really devoted to the Catholic Church, and I decided to leave it. Church just didn't seem like the place to find God.

RENEE: Really? Something like that happened to me. When I was about twelve, I looked at what my church was telling me, and I realized it was all wrong. So I chucked the whole thing. So the woods became my church, and now I come out here every so often to keep in touch with God.

DAN: To tell the truth, I'm not sure there is a God at all.

RENEE: That's why we're out here. Maybe this way you'll feel God. Remember, God is life and life is God. It's easier to see, out here, miles from any other people.

(Raucous carousing is heard offstage. Enter two BOYS, one of whom is carrying a case of beer. They are drunk.)

SECOND BOY: Hey, loser, give me another can.

FIRST BOY: Hey, look man! Like, lovers!

SECOND BOY: Oooh, stud man!

FIRST BOY *(tossing* DAN *a can of beer):* Have one on us! *(Whispers something to his friend, and they break out in loud laughter as they exit.)*

RENEE: I'm sorry about that. Nothing like that has ever happened before.

DAN: I understand.

RENEE: Okay. Now just sit there, and open yourself up, and you'll feel God.

(They sit still for a few moments, and DAN *tries to feel God. He closes his eyes and makes an earnest attempt, but he eventually becomes so self-conscious that he cannot help laughing out loud.)*

RENEE: Dan, what's so funny?

DAN: Nothing.

*(*DAN *tries again, but thunder rumbles in the distance, and rain starts to fall.)*

RENEE: Oh, shoot. Now it's beginning to rain!

*(*DAN *gets up, puts his arm around* RENEE, *and they huddle under the rain as they exit together. Lights out, then up again on Dan's* MOTHER, *who paces back and forth in agitation.)*

MOTHER: Dan, where were you? Your father and I worried all night!

DAN: I was out.

MOTHER: Out where?

DAN: Renee's house.

MOTHER: All night?

DAN: Ma, nothing happened.

MOTHER: Oh, nothing happened. What exactly does that mean?

DAN: It means nothing happened.

MOTHER: I suppose you mean you just sat up all night watching the stars? (DAN *starts to answer, but decides against it.*) Even if nothing *did* happen, what will the neighbors say?

DAN: The neighbors don't know.

MOTHER: Are you so sure? Since you weren't at church this morning, half a dozen people asked where you were. I had to tell them you weren't feeling well. That's what I've been telling them for the past three weeks, since you've stopped coming to mass. And they're starting to get concerned. Mrs. Armstrong asked if she should send flowers.

DAN: Why don't you just tell them I'm doubting the Church?

MOTHER: I can't do that!

DAN: Why not? It's the truth.

MOTHER: This is just a passing phase, anyway. Your Uncle John went through the same thing, but he came back to the Church after about two years.

DAN: You're going to tell the people at church I'm not feeling well for the next two years?

MOTHER: Of course not. I'll have to come up with something else. Is this Renee Catholic?

DAN: What does that have to do with anything?

MOTHER: What church does she go to?

DAN: She doesn't go to any church.

MOTHER: She's an atheist?

DAN: No. She believes in God. She just doesn't believe in church. And I think she's probably right. If there is a God, then he probably doesn't care—

MOTHER: What do you mean, *if* there is a God? Are you turning into an atheist, too?

DAN: I didn't mean anything—

MOTHER: Dan, what did I do wrong? I raised . . . tried to raise you to be a good Catholic man. I did my best to help you understand. I read to you from the Bible myself, I answered all your questions, sent you to Sunday school. I even bought you that children's Bible.

DAN: The children's Bible? That was probably one of the first things that turned me off toward religion.

MOTHER: Why? I thought it would be a wonderful book for you.

DAN: Did you ever look at it yourself?

MOTHER: Well, no. When I got it, you said you were too old for me to read to you, so I let you read it by yourself.

DAN: But you didn't know what it was like?

MOTHER: I never read it myself, but I assumed—

DAN: It was one of the most awful books I've ever seen. I've always wondered what could have possessed you to buy that book. What was the salesman like? Was he like this?

(*Enter a children's Bible* SALESMAN. *He is of the seedier variety of salesman, and his manner suggests a depraved purveyor of pornography. The* SALESMAN *approaches her slowly, a children's Bible under one arm, looking around to make sure no one is watching. When he reaches her, he touches her shoulder.*)

SALESMAN: Excuse me, ma'am. You look like you might have children.

MOTHER *(recoiling from his touch):* Yes, what of it?

SALESMAN *(suggestively):* Children like books, right?

MOTHER: I suppose.

SALESMAN *(even more suggestively, especially every time he says the word* pictures*):* Especially books with pictures, eh?

MOTHER: Pictures?

SALESMAN: Yes, ma'am. Pictures. I have books for sale. Books for children. Books with pictures.

MOTHER: Now, look here. I find your manner more than a little suspicious. I believe I should report your activities to the authorities. *(She starts to leave. The* SALESMAN *blocks her path and changes to honey-sweet tactics.)*

SALESMAN: Pardon me, ma'am. I don't think I have made myself clear. The books I have for sale are Bibles. Children's Bibles.

MOTHER: Children's Bibles?

SALESMAN: Yes, ma'am. The good book rewritten for the little ones. The language is simple and quite clear, and an artist's rendering accompanies every story.

MOTHER *(taken in by the new approach):* It seems I may have misjudged you, after all. May I see one of these Bibles?

SALESMAN: Most certainly. *(He hands her the Bible and looks over her shoulder as she pages through it.)* As you can see, every major passage is depicted pictorially, in living color.

MOTHER: Hmmm . . . yes. . . . *(Suddenly horrified.)* Good God! Look at that picture!

SALESMAN *(with relish):* Ah, yes. The Great Flood.

MOTHER: But doesn't this picture frighten the children?

SALESMAN: Of course! Who would not be frightened by this expertly done illustration? Men, women, even screaming children sucked under by the current!

MOTHER: But what purpose does this serve?

SALESMAN: Ma'am, it has been my experience that the best way to teach children religion is to scare it into them. Here, let me show you some of my personal favorites! *(He takes the Bible, finds the page he is looking for.)* Here it is! The Crucifixion! They did a fine job with this one, wouldn't you say? The blood on Christ's forehead is exactly the right shade of red, and the welts on his back almost rise right off the page! *(Disgusted,* MOTHER *has turned her head away from the picture. Unperturbed, the* SALESMAN *finds another page, moves around to her other side, and thrusts the picture into her face.)* Or this one! John the Baptist's head on a platter! *(*MOTHER *hides her face in her hands. Meanwhile the* SALESMAN *has found another page.)* Or King Herod's soldiers slaying every baby in Bethlehem!

MOTHER *(giving in):* All right! All right! I'll buy it! Just leave me alone!

(The SALESMAN *leaves.* MOTHER *enters her conversation with* DAN *again.)*

DAN: You can't even stand to look at the pictures yourself! How do think I felt when I was six years old and I saw them!

MOTHER: I'm sorry, Dan, I didn't know. The cover seemed innocent enough. But that isn't the impression I meant to give you about religion. I just hoped that you could find the same hope and comfort in the Church that I had.

DAN: I'm sorry, Mom. If you say your faith works for you, I'll take your word for it. It's just that I feel like I'm lying to myself when I try to believe in God, and that feeling gets worse the harder I try.

MOTHER: Would you at least indulge me a little and go to church? Act a little religious for my sake.

DAN: Okay, for the sake of argument, let's say you're right. There is a God in heaven. *(Heavenly lighting and the sounds of angelic choirs.)* I've gone to church to please you, even though I've lost my faith. What would that do to my chances for salvation?

(In this scene, MOTHER enters the fantasy as a harried bureaucrat who must contend with souls who hope to enter heaven, and DAN plays himself, after his death—one of these souls. MOTHER is sitting behind the desk, and DAN is pacing back and forth at the far end of the stage.)

MOTHER: You can come in now. We've reviewed your application.

DAN: Well, how does it look?

MOTHER: According to our records, you've kept the Sabbath holy, honored your mother and father, given of yourself, both financially and with volunteer work, to your church, the list goes on and on. . . .

DAN: So, I'll make it into heaven?

MOTHER: Well, there is one slight problem. . . .

DAN: What is it?

MOTHER: It seems that, while you have walked the straight and narrow, your heart really hasn't been in your actions.

DAN: But I've gone to church every Sunday, given money . . . it's all right there in your files. . . .

MOTHER: The problem we have is that, well . . . you did all these things for your mother, not for the Almighty.

DAN: What difference does it make? I did everything right, didn't I?

MOTHER: For someone who actually believed, your record would be exemplary. However, it is quite clear that you never did believe there is a God. You followed the letter of the law to please your mother, but you never quite caught on to its spirit.

DAN: Well, I believe now!

MOTHER: I'm afraid it's a little late for that. *Everyone* believes when they get over to this side, but it's what happens on earth, before you die, that matters.

DAN: I tried as hard as I could, but I still couldn't believe. Doesn't that count for something?

MOTHER: Your efforts certainly aren't being held against you. But instead of lying to your mother and to yourself, you should have spent those Sunday mornings at home, you should have given your money to some secular charity. . . . If you hadn't compounded your sins by being untrue to yourself and everyone around you— and, most of all, God—you might have gotten off with only a few years in purgatory. . . .

DAN: So, what's going to happen to me?

MOTHER: I have no option but to send you all the way downstairs. *(Makes a mark on a form she is holding.)*

DAN: But . . .

MOTHER: I'm terribly sorry. I don't make the rules, but I do have to follow them.

DAN: I was only trying to do the right thing!

MOTHER: There's absolutely nothing I can do. And you do know where they say the road that's paved with good intentions leads.

(DAN *and his* MOTHER *return to their own characters. Normal lighting.)*

DAN: To hell, Mom. Is that what you really want?

MOTHER: I don't understand.

DAN: What part don't you understand? Here, I'll explain it again. *(Heavenly lighting and music again, but* MOTHER *stops it almost immediately with a wave of her arm.)*

MOTHER: It's not that at all! I just don't understand what has happened to you. You're doubting the Church, staying out all night with loose girls—

DAN: Renee is not—

MOTHER: Whatever happened to Jennifer? She was such a nice girl. Maybe Father McLaughlin is right. Maybe parents need to discipline more. You're grounded for two weeks.

DAN: Ma . . .

MOTHER: Go to your room. Now!

*(*DAN *moves to the part of the stage that is his room and turns on an imaginary television. The end of a television commercial is heard, and then applause. The lights change for a fantasy scene, and* DAN *finds himself in the middle of the game show* Jeopardy! *Enter* ALEX TREBEK, *host of* Jeopardy! JENNIFER, *and* RENEE. DAN *joins them behind the contestants' table, and* ALEX *stands behind the host's podium.)*

ALEX: Welcome back to *Jeopardy!* ladies and gentlemen, and we're in the middle of a very close match. Before we get back to the game, let's find out a little bit about today's players. We'll start with you, Jennifer.

JENNIFER: My name is Jennifer Gustavson, I enjoy singing in the choir and going to church, and I'm a Catholic. *(Applause is heard.)*

RENEE: I'm Renee Billings, I'm into meditation and New Age philosophy, and I'm a nondenominational transcendentalist. *(Applause.)*

DAN: I'm Dan Wilson, I enjoy archery, and . . . I'm undecided about my religion. *(Silence—no applause.* ALEX *clears his throat judgmentally.)*

ALEX: Moving on, it's time for the Final Jeopardy round, and the topic is world religion. Our players have made their wagers, so the Final Jeopardy answer is this: "Of all the world's religions, this is the one with all the answers." (JENNIFER *starts writing right away.)* All right, contestants, you have one minute to come up with the Final Jeopardy question. (Jeopardy! *music plays briefly, while* RE- NEE *writes down her answer.* JENNIFER *finishes almost immediately and looks around, obviously very sure of her answer.* DAN *doesn't write anything. Music stops.)* Time's up, so let's see what the con- testants have chosen for their questions.

JENNIFER: What is Roman Catholicism?

RENEE: What is Buddhism?

DAN: No guess.

ALEX: And the Final Jeopardy question is . . . "What is goiter?" One moment, ladies and gentlemen, I believe this is a question from the last round. Let me see . . . *(Searches frantically though the cards, spewing them everywhere.)*

PRODUCER *(offstage):* Stop the tape.

ALEX: Can you get Vic down here? He's the one who does the research. Maybe he'll know.

PRODUCER *(after a pause):* Vic's not available. You'll have to make something up.

ALEX: Make something up?

PRODUCER: I'm sorry, Alex, but we're backlogged two weeks, what with Teen Week plus the regular schedule. We don't have time to look up the answer. Just make something up. Roll tape.

ALEX *(regaining composure):* Well, I'm afraid all three contestants were wrong. It was sort of a trick question. It was: "What is none of them?" So be sure to tune in tomorrow when . . . *(Everyone fades offstage but* DAN, *who returns to his seat. New Age music plays on the television for a moment, and an announcer's voice is heard.)*

ANNOUNCER: Dianetics. By L. Ron Hubbard.

*(*DAN *turns off the television, then hears a tapping, like small stones lightly striking a window.* DAN *wakes up and goes to an imaginary window. He sees* RENEE.*)*

DAN: Renee, why are you throwing rocks at my window? Are you trying to break it?

RENEE: I was trying to get your attention. I tried calling you, but your mother said you couldn't come to the phone because you're grounded. Is that true? *(*DAN *nods.)* Why?

DAN: Because I didn't let my parents know where I was when I stayed at your place on Saturday.

RENEE: Was that a disaster, or what? I just dropped by to see what you thought of all that.

DAN: Since then I've decided there is no God. Inside or outside of church.

RENEE *(a little disappointed):* Oh. I guess it's hard to feel in touch with God when you get rained on and insulted by drunks. . . .

DAN: I'm sorry.

RENEE: Hey, don't apologize. It's the way you feel. Nothing to be sorry for. So . . . how long are you grounded?

DAN: Two weeks. I get out tomorrow, though. I have a job interview. I want to be a counselor at Scout camp.

RENEE: The Boy Scouts? You better watch out. I heard a couple years ago that they kicked one kid out of the Boy Scouts because he was an atheist.

DAN: Really? I didn't know that. I just hope no religion questions come up.

RENEE: What if they do come up? What will you say?

DAN: I'll try to cover it up somehow.

(A knock on DAN's door is heard.)

MOTHER (from offstage): Dan, who are you talking to?

DAN: Myself, Ma. (To RENEE:) Wish me luck for Thursday.

RENEE: Good luck. Peace.

DAN: Peace.

(DAN falls asleep. Enter JENNIFER, FATHER MCLAUGHLIN, Dan's MOTHER, VIRGIL, and DANTE. DANTE is a gawking tourist dressed in a Hawaiian shirt, and VIRGIL is dressed in a suit, like a museum tour guide.)

DANTE: Hey, Virgil, are we about through with this "Inferno" place?

VIRGIL: This very chamber in which we now stand is the Fourth Ring of the Ninth Circle, the final stop on the Inferno portion of the Divine Comedy Guided Tour. This, my friend, is the eternal home of the committers of the most treasonous transgressions. These souls are the most treacherous trash ever to tread the earth.

DANTE (indicating something offstage): Wow, man, look! Who are those two guys, hanging upside down up there?

VIRGIL: Those pathetic human pendulums are the souls of Cassius and Brutus, devious dealers in deceit, damned for their designs in the dethroning and death of their lord Julius Caesar.

JENNIFER, MOTHER, and FATHER (with interest): Ohhhhh.

DANTE *(waving to them):* How d'you do? My name's Dante Alighieri. I'm not dead, you know.

VIRGIL: If you would step this way, please.

DANTE: Yeah, sure. *(Raises his camera to take a picture of Caesar and Brutus.)* Say cheese.

VIRGIL: No flash pictures, please.

DANTE: Sorry. *(Noticing something else offstage.)* Wow, check that out, too! Who's that one—the one with his head between his knees, puking all over his feet?

VIRGIL: That, sir, is Judas Iscariot, the apostle who received in return for the betrayal of his Christ a handful of silver and eternal condemnation.

JENNIFER, MOTHER, and FATHER *(with contempt):* Ohhhhh.

DANTE: Glad to meet you, Mr. Iscariot. Holy balls! *(Pointing at DAN.)* How'd they get his body to do *that?*

FATHER: What did he do to deserve such a fate?

JENNIFER: He looks kind of familiar . . .

VIRGIL: This wretch of wretches, Daniel Wilson . . .

JENNIFER, MOTHER, and FATHER *(with horror):* Ohhhhh!

VIRGIL: . . . committed the worst sin of all. By rejecting his own mother, who bore him into the mortal world, and rejecting our Lord Jesus Christ, he performed that vilest act—making the neighbors talk! Only confinement in the coldest corner can compensate for the condemnable crime that he has committed.

JENNIFER: I told you you thought too much!

FATHER: Lack of discipline, lack of discipline . . .

MOTHER: Oh, Dan! What will people say when they find out you ended up here!

(DANTE *shakes his head and whistles.*)

VIRGIL: This concludes the Inferno portion of our tour. In fifteen minutes we will ascend to Purgatorio, and if you need to use the rest room, it's down that hall and to the right.

DANTE (*to* DAN *and the other inmates of hell*): So long! Maybe I'll write a book about you someday!

(*All but* DAN *exit, an alarm clock rings,* DAN *wakes up, and his* MOTHER *enters and helps him put on a tie. The* SCOUT INTERVIEWER *enters and crosses to his desk. Dan's* MOTHER *exits, and* DAN *crosses to the* INTERVIEWER's *desk.*)

INTERVIEWER (*consulting application*): You're Daniel R. Wilson?

DAN: Yes, sir.

INTERVIEWER: Very good. So, tell me, why do you want to be a counselor at summer camp?

DAN: Well, two other scouts in my troop worked at camp last summer, and they said it was enjoyable and rewarding.

INTERVIEWER: And where were you thinking of working at camp?

DAN: Either the archery range or the swimming beach, I suppose. Archery and lifesaving were my two favorite merit badges.

INTERVIEWER: Will you be able to handle institutional food for two months?

DAN: I'm sure I'll learn how.

INTERVIEWER (*looking at application a little more closely*): I see you didn't answer one of the questions—"What does the statement 'A Scout is reverent' mean to you?" Was this an oversight?

DAN: No, I just wasn't sure how to answer it when I filled it out.

INTERVIEWER: Surely you had ample time to think the question through.

DAN: Actually, at the time I filled out the application, I was reexamining my religious beliefs, so I didn't answer it.

INTERVIEWER: That's certainly very understandable. Adolescence is a time when one must look at one's life and make choices about the kind of man he will be. Do you have everything sorted out now?

DAN: Yes, I do.

INTERVIEWER: I'm happy to hear that, because it is my understanding of the Scout Law that a reverent Scout is one who is firm in his beliefs. Devoutness is the greatest form of strength, I always say. I'd like to hear what came of your period of readjustment.

DAN: I guess you could say I became a devout atheist.

INTERVIEWER: Pardon me?

DAN: I'm a devout atheist.

INTERVIEWER: Do you truly understand what that word means?

DAN: Yes.

INTERVIEWER: Tell me, then. What does it mean when you say you are an atheist?

DAN: I don't believe in God.

INTERVIEWER: You don't believe in God. You *don't* believe in God. Tell me, Daniel, if you don't believe in God, how can you be a good Scout?

DAN: Pardon me?

INTERVIEWER: If you don't believe in God, how can you be a good Scout? If you don't believe in God, what is there to be reverent toward?

DAN: My beliefs.

INTERVIEWER: Your beliefs. If you don't believe in God, what is it you do believe?

DAN: I believe people do not have immortal souls. I believe death is the final end. I believe it is possible to be a good person without believing in some divine power.

INTERVIEWER: And I believe we may have no position for you. When you get home, please read the Scout Law. It's twelfth point is "A Scout is reverent: A Scout is reverent toward God and faithful in his religious duties." It does not say, "A Scout is reverent only if he feels like believing in God." It is quite clear. If that is all, I think we can draw this interview to a close.

DAN: Before I go, I'd just like to say that the same point of the Scout Law says Scouts should respect others' beliefs. I really don't think you have lived up to the Scout Law any better than I have.

(The INTERVIEWER exits, and DAN is left alone onstage. He walks away from the area representing the interviewer's office, loosening his tie, and RENEE enters. They hug.)

RENEE: So, how did the interview go?

DAN: I don't think it went all that badly.

RENEE: So you'll get the job?

DAN: No, I'm not going to get the job, but it still went well.

RENEE: I don't get it.

DAN: Remember when I said that I'd probably try to wiggle out of any religion questions if they came up? Well, some religion questions did come up, and I didn't hide. I stood my ground, and I felt good about it. I decided that if he refused me the job because of my atheism, it would be more his loss than mine, since he'd be losing a damn good counselor.

RENEE: I'm happy to hear that it all worked out, then.

DAN: Yeah. Actually, I shouldn't be here, because I'm still grounded. My mother let me out this morning so I could go to the interview, and she probably still thinks I'm there.

RENEE: Is your mother still mad at you?

DAN: I don't think she's mad, really. Just upset because she doesn't understand why I don't believe in God. I've decided I'll try to tell her in her own terms. You see, her favorite part of the Bible was always the parables, so I thought I might tell her a parable of my own. . . .

(DAN *delivers the following speech as a peaceful Christ would have told the parables—not as a Bible-thumping fire-and-brimstone preacher, but as a calm, reserved speaker. His* MOTHER *enters and sits at his feet, as if she were one of his disciples, eager to hear him speak.*)

DAN: Gather around, and I will tell you why I ceased to believe.

RENEE: Please tell us your tale!

MOTHER: Please tell us your tale!

DAN: The story begins when I was a young boy, before I saw the light. Unquestioningly, I accepted the teachings of my church, much as the grazing lamb, who concentrates on the grass immediately before its nose. But the lamb will pause occasionally and look up from the grass it is eating. I looked around and saw flocks of lambs other than my own feeding off of other patches of grass. I saw the flocks of the non-Catholic Christians, the flock of the Jewish people, flocks of Buddhists, Hindus, Muslims, flocks too numerous to mention. And while their grass was different, it seemed to nourish them as well as my own grass nourished me.

MOTHER: So, the grass of the unbelievers looked more appealing than your own and you joined their flock.

DAN: Alas, that is not so. When I realized that mine was not the only flock, I began to look closely at my own grass and, more importantly, question why I was eating it. I found that I dressed up, listened to mass, behaved myself, and ate this particular grass not because it was what God wanted, but because it was what my *mother* wanted.

MOTHER: But was not your mother a wise and loving person?

DAN: Yes, that she was, as most mothers are. But I needed to find my own answers, I needed to discover for myself the sweetest patch of grass. So I climbed the highest mountain I could find so I could ask God personally which grass was most palatable. I reached the summit of the mountain and cried my question out to the wind. I listened intently for the softest whispering of the wind, the faintest flutter within my own soul. Not a word did I hear.

MOTHER: Is this when you saw the light?

DAN: Yes, except it was more of a darkness.

MOTHER: Do you not despair in your disbelief? Do you not hunger for the grass from time to time?

DAN: From time to time I indeed do. But I find that no matter how hard I try, I cannot chew the grass, and I spit it out before I can swallow. For now I realize that I am not a lamb but a man, and I must eat the food of men.

(MOTHER *touches* DAN *tenderly on the shoulder and then exits.*)

RENEE: I just wish there were some way I could help you find God.

DAN: I know. That's what my mother wants, and it's what Jennifer wanted, but I don't think anyone can help me. *(Pause.)* I haven't stopped looking, you know. Last night, I decided to give God one last chance. As I lay there in bed, I said out loud, to the air around me, "God, do you exist?" And the air didn't answer.

RENEE: Maybe you weren't listening hard enough.

DAN: Maybe so. Well, I've got to go. Peace.

RENEE: Peace.

(Blackout.)

ROBERT KERR

And the Air Didn't Answer has a rather convoluted history. It was born at the Young Playwrights Summer Conference in St. Paul, a five-page play structured as a dialogue between Dan and his mother, who played the roles in the fantasy scenes. The second draft introduced the characters of Jennifer and Renee, as well as several new fantasy scenes, and it was the one I entered for the Young Playwrights Festival. During the winter, having more or less forgotten about the festival, I worked some more on the script with the help of the Young Playwrights program affiliated with the Playwrights Center in Minneapolis. I returned to the original two-character format, and this version was performed in the one-act festival at my high school. The following spring I found I was a finalist in the Festival and synthesized the two-character version from the past winter and the version I had first sent in for the Festival. I made some more changes and cuts prior to the full production in the fall, one year and some months after I first started writing the play.

In short, I learned that playwrights use a lot of paper. Looking at the size of the stack of plot outlines, scenes that were cut, scenes that never made it into the play, and pages that got jammed in the printer, I feel certain that I am single-handedly responsible for the destruction of an entire forest.

The cycle has begun again. Since the Festival, in my spare time at Macalester College in St. Paul, I have completed a first draft of a one-act black comedy, *Finnegan's Funeral Parlor and Ice Cream Shoppe,* and have started working on a musical tentatively titled *Charlie Chapleman, Boy President.* I am also polishing some short stories I have written over the past two years, and I think I feel a novel coming on.

I'd like to thank the actors—Richard Council for his booming, capricious God, Jihmi Kennedy for his menacing Crusader, John Augustine for his slimy Salesman, Jill Tasker for a prim Jennifer, Erica Gimpel for her free-spirited Renee, Debra Monk for her bewildered yet loving Mother, and Robert Sean Leonard for the definitive Dan. Also, many thanks to everyone else who helped, especially the director, Christopher Durang. I can't think of a more appropriate person to direct this play.

And I dedicate this play to Julie Schmidt and Dallas Brunson, who brought it to life in the first place.

EBONY

by Pamela Mariva Mshana
(age sixteen when play was written)
Ontario, California

NOTE:
For the purpose of publication in this collection, certain words
have been changed by the playwright, and some profanity has been
deleted from the working script of the play as performed at Playwrights Horizons, New York City, October 4 through 8, 1987.

Ebony was first performed as part of the Chapman readings series at Playwrights Horizons on October 4, 1987. The reading was directed by Sheldon Epps. Elan Garonzik was the playwright adviser. The cast:

EBONY	Erica Gimpel
LINDA, *her mother*	Lorraine Toussaint
DOC, *her mother's current husband*	James McDaniel
LISA, *her cousin*	Valerie Evering
YOUNG EBONY	Amber Kain
BRENDA, *her auntie*	Olivia Virgil Harper
KENTRELLE, *her friend*	Toni Ann Johnson
DAD, *her stepfather*	Victor Love
DICE, *her first boyfriend*	Erik King

SETTING:

Act One: The stage is divided into two areas: the living room and child's bedroom area of a lower-middle-class home. The bedroom is noticeably better kept than the living room. The front and kitchen doors open out from the living room.

Act Two: The living room area of a middle-middle-class home. Action also takes place in Ebony's childhood bedroom from Act One.

ACT ONE

At rise, EBONY *is in her bedroom writing in her diary. Her* MOTHER *is in the living room watching TV.* DOC *walks through the front door, just coming home from work.*

DOC: I'm home.

LINDA: Hello, honey.

DOC: Hi. You sure are an ugly sight for a man to see after work.

(LINDA *pats her head, stuffs some hair under her scarf.*)

LINDA *(laughing):* Oh, I haven't dressed yet.

DOC *(looking at his watch):* Well, it's five o'clock, no need to get dressed now. (DOC *exits into kitchen. Offstage:*) This place is a mess. Don't you do anything around here? Just look at this! A sink full of dishes, the floor is so sticky I'm scared to walk on it, and I had to wear a dirty shirt to work today because you never do the wash. What's happening to you? You look so dirty, I don't even want to kiss you, much less make love to you.

LINDA: Well, you know I haven't been feeling well.

DOC: Woman, you've been moping around here claiming sick for two months now. You done lost your job and your mind if you think I'm gonna keep living this way. I'm tired of it.

(EBONY *looks up from her diary.*)

LINDA: Well, you ain't exactly the kind of man that encourages a woman to be all fixed up when her man gets home. You treat me like dirt. What do you expect me to look like?

DOC: What do I expect you to look like? Well, if you're not dressed up, I would expect you to at least look a little like a woman.

LINDA: Are you saying I'm not a woman?

DOC: You said it, not me.

LINDA: You might as well have said it.

DOC: Are you gonna cook some dinner?

LINDA: Are you sure I'm woman enough to do it?

DOC: Look, don't start with me. If you want to be treated like a woman by me, put a little more effort in this relationship, and for God's sake clean yourself up. I don't work as hard as I do to have you sitting around here looking as cheap as you do, filling your head with soaps and gossip on the phone. You better start doing something about—

(EBONY *slams her pencil down.*)

EBONY *(offstage):* Mom!?

LINDA: Yeah, Ebony.

EBONY: Come here.

(LINDA *starts to Ebony's room while* DOC *is still talking.* DOC *follows her.*)

LINDA: Yeah, Ebony?

EBONY: Why don't you guys keep it down if you absolutely have to argue every day? It's driving me crazy hearing that crap. Every day the exact same argument. Then you guys make up.

DOC: Look, woman, don't walk away from me when I'm talking to you. . . .

LINDA: Ebony called me. . . .

DOC: I don't care if God in heaven called you, don't walk away from me when I'm talking to you.

LINDA: Yeah, sure, Doc . . . whatever . . . Ebony, as we were saying?

(DOC *slaps* LINDA *down.*)

EBONY: Mom! Doc, what's wrong with you? Why don't you get out of our lives . . . ?

LINDA *(crying):* Ebony! Don't . . .

DOC: You know, Linda, as hard as I try for you, you've got a whole lot of nerve getting smart with me.

EBONY: Who's talking about nerve? Mom, now do you see what I've been telling you is true? I told you you guys were gonna keep on until he starts hitting you, and I just don't understand it. I'd just leave him.

DOC *(laughing):* She wouldn't leave me.

EBONY: Oh, wouldn't she? Mom, tell him you will. Let him know where you stand. *(Pause.)* Mom . . . tell him.

(DOC *laughs again, looks at* EBONY, *then goes to* LINDA *and helps her up on the side of the bed.*)

DOC: Baby, you wouldn't leave Doc, would you? (LINDA*'s silent. She's trying to stop crying.* EBONY *stares at them in disgust)* Linda, honey, you'll always be my woman, won't you? *(He wipes her tears.)* I'm sorry, Linda. (LINDA *smiles at him.*)

EBONY: Oh, my God. Ma, don't let him talk you into it again. It's all gonna happen again tomorrow.

DOC: Linda, you wouldn't ever leave me, would you?

LINDA *(smiling):* No, Doc, I wouldn't ever leave you.

(EBONY *turns away.*)

DOC: I knew you'd stay with me. We'll make it, baby. (DOC *starts out, then stops and taps* EBONY *on the shoulder.* EBONY *turns.*) She ain't never gonna leave me, but you . . . feel free anytime.

EBONY: Get out of my room.

DOC: Ot, ot, ah—I pay the rent here, and I'm leaving because everything is under control, not because of you. (DOC *exits.*)

EBONY: Mom, I just don't get it.

LINDA: Ebony, I already know this speech.

EBONY: Why do you let him talk to you like that? And even this time hit you? Is this what you guys call the beginning of a new relationship? I mean, don't you like a man that talks to you softly and treats you gentle, sneaks up on you and gives hugs and kisses?

LINDA: Yeah, I like those things, but where is this man? Sometimes you have to settle for a man that tries. You know, you sound a lot like me when I was younger, but you'll learn. Men are so unpredictable, and maybe you don't understand Doc. He's gentle in his own way.

EBONY: His way wouldn't satisfy me.

LINDA: You are so set in your ways. Listen to me, there's *not* such a man.

EBONY: Or maybe you never found him because you're too quick to settle for something else.

LINDA: Ebony, you never accept that I've been where you're going.

EBONY: You never accept that you and I are two very different people. You always want to protect me from your mistakes. Let me live my life.

LINDA: You see? You haven't heard a word I've said. You're too tied up in what you believe. Why can't you just take my word?

EBONY: Because some things people have to learn on their own, make their own mistakes. I'm me and I don't think like you.

LINDA: Look, don't get smart.

EBONY: Oh, God! Every time I tell you my feelings, you say I'm getting smart.

LINDA: It's some things you don't say to your mother! *(She pauses, thinking, then speaks more softly to* EBONY.) Anyway, you're too young to understand why. I know this doesn't sound right, but, Ebony, it's for you. This is the only way I can keep a roof over your head. You know I'm not working and—I don't expect you to understand now. One day you will.

EBONY *(confused and yelling):* All for me! Understand! Oh, I understand. I understand that you get beat and yelled at every day, I understand that you're a sucker for him, but all for me.

LINDA *(angry):* Yes! All for you! Why else do you think I'm here? And don't you ever in your life say that I'm a sucker for any man! I'm a sucker for you, and you better start watching how you talk to me.

EBONY: Forget it, Mom. If I can't speak the truth, it's no use for me to say anything. Just forget we had this conversation. I'm sorry I asked about you and Doc.

LINDA: Don't tell me to forget it. You know I hate when you say forget it.

EBONY: Look, you've turned a simple question into a big argument. Can't we just let it go?

LINDA: No, we can't. (EBONY *hums as her mother talks.)* You always start something and blame it on me. If you'd just listen, you'd see I'm right.

EBONY: You're right says who? And I'm always wrong? Don't you think I know how I feel?

LINDA: You know, you *are* right, let's do forget it, 'cause you're so defensive, nothing I say you listen to anyway. You make your own mistakes.

(LINDA *exits, slamming the door.* EBONY *gets her diary and starts to write.*)

EBONY: Dear Diary, life is hopeless. You're always fighting to get through something, and when you do, there's always something else to fight. My life has gotten to the point that there's nothing happy about it. Life is upside down and it has been trying to get to me to make me crack up or something. Life took my father away when I was young, and it's been taking things ever since. Oh yeah, but that's life. I feel like I'm going crazy. Ebony is sick in the head. You know why I feel this way? Because I've had a crazy life. I remember when I was younger, I guess I was about eight. I seriously thought I was evil. Everybody told me I was, and as a young girl I believed it. Once I had a fight . . .

(*A light change establishes the past downstage in the living room. Ebony's* AUNTIE BRENDA *is there.* EBONY *looks on in a daze as a bratty-looking little girl,* LISA, *runs onstage, with blood falling from her mouth, and* YOUNG EBONY *follows her in.*)

LISA (*crying*): Mommy, Mommy!

BRENDA: What happened?

LISA: Ebony pushed me in the bathtub and broke my tooth.

BRENDA (*looking at* YOUNG EBONY): Why'd you do that?

YOUNG EBONY (*scared but honest*): I didn't try to break her tooth, I just pushed her, and that's where she fell. We were fighting and *she* started it. She took my dollar and wouldn't give it back.

BRENDA (*yelling*): I'll be glad when your momma come home. Every time I baby-sit you, you cause trouble, you evil little witch.

YOUNG EBONY: I'm sorry.

BRENDA: I bet you are after you broke my little girl's tooth. (YOUNG EBONY *sits, crying.*) Hush up! You ain't hurt, my girl is. *(To* LISA:*)* Come on, baby, Mommy will fix it.

(BRENDA *and* LISA *exit.* EBONY *watches the* YOUNG EBONY *cry.*)

YOUNG EBONY: God, I don't want to be evil. Will you take me so I don't have to hurt anyone anymore? I'm sorry, God.

(LISA *enters holding a towel to her mouth.*)

LISA: Look a here, the evil girl is trying to pray. Well, God doesn't hear evil people's prayers.

YOUNG EBONY: I'm not evil!

LISA: Yes, you are, 'cause my momma said you are. She said you're a witch, you're hateful, and you're the evilest girl we know. You're probably the devil's daughter. I'm going to leave, I'm scared of you.

(LISA *exits. There is a knock at the door as the lights cross-fade back to the present.*)

BOTH EBONYS: Who is it?

KENTRELLE: It's Kentrelle.

BOTH EBONYS: Come in.

(KENTRELLE *enters.*)

YOUNG EBONY: Hi, Kentrelle.

(KENTRELLE *can't see* YOUNG EBONY.)

KENTRELLE *(to older* EBONY): What's wrong with you? You look like you've been crying.

BOTH EBONYS: Kentrelle, did you know you are my best friend in the whole world?

KENTRELLE: Yeah, you told me that years ago. Hey, what's with you, aren't you going to the party?

(The lights go out on YOUNG EBONY.*)*

EBONY: Oh yeah, the party.

KENTRELLE: Oh yeah, the party. This is only the biggest party of the year. Girl, whatever you've been taking, you've had enough. I don't know what's got into you lately, but snap out of it quick 'cause I'm ready to go.

EBONY: Let me get my coat. *(She gets her coat. They both start to exit.)* I hope this party is fun.

(The past lights come up downstage, and BRENDA *enters with* LISA.*)*

BRENDA: It won't be fun. You're not going to any party.

*(*EBONY *turns, sees* BRENDA, *and gets a scared look on her face.)*

EBONY: My mother told you I could go to the party.

*(*KENTRELLE *can't see* BRENDA *or* LISA *and thinks* EBONY *is talking to her.)*

KENTRELLE *(confused):* Your mother didn't tell me anything. Who cares about her, anyway?

BRENDA: You should have told me you were leaving.

LISA: Yeah, you should have told her.

EBONY: Oh, I'm sorry. I just forgot because we were late.

KENTRELLE *(confused):* No kidding we're late.

BRENDA: Well, now you're not going.

EBONY: Yes I am, my mother said I could.

KENTRELLE: Will you forget about your mother and come on?

(EBONY *starts to leave.* BRENDA *pulls her back.* KENTRELLE *sees* EBONY *jerk back.*)

BRENDA: You're not going to the party.

KENTRELLE: What are you doing?

EBONY: Kentrelle, you go ahead. I have to do something before I go. I'll be there later.

KENTRELLE: Are you okay?

EBONY: Yeah. I'll be there later.

KENTRELLE: Okay, but I'll be looking for you. (KENTRELLE *exits.*)

EBONY: Let go of me, Brenda, you're hurting my arm.

BRENDA: That's what I'm trying to do, just like you hurt my little girl's tooth. (BRENDA *twists* EBONY'*s arm.*)

EBONY: Brenda, if you don't stop, I'm gonna hit you back.

BRENDA: Oh, you gonna hit me back, then do it.

LISA: You better not hit my momma.

(BRENDA *twists* EBONY'*s arm again.* EBONY *kicks her, and* BRENDA *falls.*)

BRENDA: You little . . .

LISA: Get her, Mommy.

(BRENDA *starts hitting* EBONY *on the head.*)

BRENDA: So, you still think you're going, huh?

EBONY (*crying*): Stop, Brenda, stop, stop, Brenda! I'm sorry.

(LISA *laughs.*)

BRENDA: I told your momma when you were born you wasn't nothing but trouble. I never wanted a niece anyway, just another whiny kid for the adults to put off on me, much less a niece like you, a evil little witch.

EBONY (*yelling*): I'm not evil! (*Now* BRENDA *stops hitting* EBONY, *and* LISA *stops laughing.* BRENDA *takes* LISA's *hand, and they exit.* EBONY *goes to her room, stops crying, and takes up her diary.*) Diary, that was the beginning of a new Ebony—a scared child that wanted to prove she wasn't evil. I tried hard during those days not to fight and to read children's Bibles, praying I wasn't the witch my auntie said I was. I used to love being with my father. I never felt evil around him. He used to call me Princess, and I'd forget about being a witch. But nothing good ever lasts for long in my life.

(*The lights cross-fade back into the past.* DAD *enters.*)

DAD: Hello, princess.

EBONY: Hi, Daddy, are we still going to the movies tonight?

DAD: No. Let's stay here and look at the photo albums.

EBONY: That'll be fun, I'll get them off my shelf. (EBONY *gets them, and they open one.*) Look, Daddy, that's when we were at Universal Studios and I thought the wax man touched me and you wouldn't believe me.

DAD (*cutting in, laughing*): And it turned out that the man was real.

EBONY: Yeah.

DAD: Look, that's your fifth birthday. I always made sure I was right next to you in your birthday pictures, I was by your side every year watching you grow up.

EBONY: You know, Daddy, it's strange, but that's the furthest back I can remember you on my birthdays.

DAD: Yeah, it is strange. You were probably too young. *(He turns the page.)*

EBONY: Daddy, this is when I was turning three. Where were you then?

DAD: You know, I don't really remember, ah . . .

EBONY: Daddy, you're not telling me the truth. Where were you?

DAD: Ebony, I want to give you something first, then I'll tell you. *(He takes a small box from his pocket and gives it to her.)*

EBONY: It's a ring, and it says, "Love." Daddy, I know you love me.

DAD: I just don't want you to forget.

EBONY: How can I forget my father loves me?

DAD *(hesitating):* 'Cause I got to leave.

EBONY: You always leave with your job.

DAD: Ebony, will you promise not to cry? I'm gonna tell you why you only remember me at that birthday and not before.

EBONY: I promise.

DAD: Ebony, I—I married your mother when you were four. I'm not your natural father.

EBONY: Yes you are, what are you talking about?

DAD: Ebony, let me finish. Your real father died two months after you were born and your mother thought it was best not to tell you, since you were too young to remember, but . . .

(EBONY *starts crying.* DAD *stops looking at her. He puts his head down.*)

DAD: But I thought I should tell you and—I still love you, you're my princess. I'm only telling you because I love you. I try not to think you're not my own. You see, love makes us real, not blood.

EBONY *(trying not to cry):* Yeah, I guess so. I just wish you hadn't told me. I mean, I love you the same, but I want your blood too. You're a king in my eyes, and that's what made me a princess. *(She hugs him.)* I love you, Daddy. *(She stops crying.)*

DAD: I love you too. *(He gently pushes her away.)* But I still have to go.

EBONY: When will you be back?

DAD: Ebony, I know this is a bad time to tell you this, but Mommy and I are getting a divorce.

EBONY: But why?

DAD: Ebony, you know we don't get along, we're always fighting.

EBONY: Daddy, please don't go.

DAD: I've got to. Please understand. I hate to see my princess cry. You'll make Daddy cry.

EBONY: I don't want to make you cry, Daddy. I just started looking at the pictures, and you're no longer at my side. What will I do without you, Daddy?

DAD: I don't know what I'll do without you either, but I've got to go. 'Bye, Princess. *(He kisses her.)*

EBONY *(trying not to cry):* 'Bye, Daddy. *(She puts on the ring and closes the door behind him.)* I love you, Daddy. . . . *(She repeats the last line till she gets angry.)* God, it's your fault, you took my real father. I wish I had my real father. I wish he was here. *(She looks up at the light bulb in her bedroom lamp. In it she sees an image of what she believes to be her real father.)* Daddy, Daddy, is that you? *(The light bulb brightens.* EBONY *touches it and burns her hand, then the light bulb gets dim again.)* Ouch! Just a plain old light bulb. It's not my father, just a plain old light bulb. *(The lights cross-fade back to the present, and* EBONY *picks up her diary.)* Diary, it was three years before I saw that man again. He didn't even call once. And I guess he forgot Christmas and my birthday too. And after three years he asked me, do I still love him? You know what I said? I said no! I said, "After three years, hey! I don't know what love is." I guess I told him. *(Chuckles.)* Well, so much for dear old Dad. *(Pause.)* I kind of got over him quick anyway. I decided to replace him with a boyfriend.

(There is a knock at the door as the lights cross-fade back into the past.)

EBONY *(yelling):* Who is it?

DICE: It's Dice, is Marc there?

EBONY: I can't hear you.

(DICE enters.)

DICE: Is Marc here? We got to go to practice.

EBONY: Oh, ah, no, he's not here. I'm his sister, Ebony. Want me to tell him something for you?

DICE: Naw, I'll see him at practice. Marc didn't tell me he had such a pretty sister.

EBONY: Thanks. He didn't tell me he had such a handsome friend.

DICE: How old are you?

EBONY: Sixteen. And you?

DICE: Nineteen. Three years ain't bad, is it?

EBONY: No, it's not bad, but what do you mean?

DICE: I want you to be my lady.

EBONY: Don't you have to go to practice?

DICE: Yeah, but I want you to answer me first.

EBONY: Boy, I just met you.

DICE: So, you like me so far, don't you?

EBONY: Maybe, but I still don't know you.

DICE: Okay, I'm Diceare Gasaveai. They call me Dice for short. My father is French and my mother is black. I play football. I'm an only child, and my family does pretty well for itself. I drive a black Nissan truck and I have a date Friday night with a girl I just met named Ebony.

EBONY: Oh yeah, where does she live?

DICE: Come on, you keep saying you don't know me. How will you know me if you don't go out with me? Please, Friday night? I know this great party we could go to. You're making me late for practice.

EBONY: I'm not making you late, go on.

DICE: I'm not gonna leave until you answer me.

EBONY: Well . . . I guess so.

DICE *(smiles):* I'll see you Friday at seven o'clock.

(DICE *exits.* EBONY *twirls into her room, grabs her diary and writes.*)

EBONY *(excited):* Oh, my God! A football player—nineteen years old—a college man with his own car interested in me! And he is fine. He even has a special air, and I love men with airs, men that's different from all the rest. Like my old stepfather. Just by being with Dice for that short time I was able to see a few qualities he had just like my old stepfather—very clean, intelligent, and sure of himself. Oh! Friday night, I can't wait, I'm gonna go crazy, what will I wear? *(She goes to her closet and looks through it, then she stops.)* My red dress. *(She takes it out, then puts it on and looks at herself in the mirror.)* Got to lose a couple of pounds before Friday. And this hair. *(She sits in front of the mirror and combs her hair.)* I know, I'll put it up. *(She puts it up and stands up and looks at herself again.)* Yeah. (EBONY *goes to the closet and gets her red shoes. She looks in the mirror and touches herself softly around the neck.)* And last . . . I'll use some of my mother's perfume.

(BRENDA *and* LISA *enter.)*

BRENDA: Don't bother, you're not going to any party.

LISA: Yeah, you don't deserve to go to a party. You're evil. You don't deserve Dice.

BRENDA: You don't deserve anybody and you'll be sorry if you go out Friday, you witch.

EBONY: But I want to go to the party.

BRENDA: Stay home, you devil.

LISA: Yeah, stay home.

(BRENDA *and* LISA *keep saying, "Stay home,"* EBONY *gets confused.)*

EBONY: Stop it! I am going out Friday, I am.

(Blackout. Lights up in the present. DICE *and* EBONY *are sitting on the bed in Ebony's room with papers in their hands.)*

DICE: Hey, that was good poetry.

EBONY: Thank you.

DICE: Okay, now that we have been to a party, out to dinner, a short drive here, and we have read a few nice poems, what do you want to do?

EBONY: Talk. You know, getting to know each other.

DICE: Ha, ha, you've got to be kidding, right?

EBONY: Ha, no, I'm not kidding.

DICE: Oh, I see, it's okay. *(He puts his arm around her and rubs the side of her arm.)* I understand if you want to take your time.

EBONY: To do what?

DICE: Look now, you know good and well what I'm talking about. Surprise! We're here all alone, if you haven't noticed.

EBONY: Yeah, I've noticed and I don't care.

(He sees EBONY is angry. He puts his hands on her face and starts to talk to her more softly.)

DICE: I'm sorry, I guess I got the wrong impression.

EBONY: Yeah, I guess you did.

(Pause. Then DICE looks at her.)

DICE: You know, you just don't look as innocent as you're making out to be. You look like if I took it real slow and rubbed your body with my love touch, you'd get *hot* just like any other girl and you'd get greedy and want me just as bad as I want you. You're not so pure in a lily-white dress sitting up on some pedestal. You got a little devil in you, too, and I know you want me, so why don't you just give it up?

EBONY: You know, I do want you, but I'm not going to make love with you. I want to be good. It seems like I never have been before.

DICE: Well, don't start now! Baby, you din already did wrong 'cause you was thinking it and that's a sin. *(He starts undoing her dress.)* You see, you might as well go all the way. I know it's your first time *doing,* but you had to be *thinking* a long time. And the best thing about it is you're doing it with me. Now, relax. I'll get you in the mood.

(BRENDA, LISA, and DAD enter as DICE kisses EBONY and lays her on the bed.)

LISA *(disgusted):* Mommy, told you you'd be sorry.

BRENDA: Evil little girl. Shame.

DAD: I'll always love you, Princess.

(Slow fade to blackout as EBONY gives in to DICE.)

ACT TWO

The living room area of a middle-middle-class home. This is where
EBONY *and* DICE *live. In general, the furnishings are of higher qual-*
ity than those in Act One.

Action also takes place in EBONY's *childhood bedroom area.*
EBONY *is pregnant, sitting in the living room.*
Lights up.

EBONY: Dear Diary, I am sorry I went out with Dice that Friday.
I'm pregnant now. When Dice found out, he asked me to marry
him, and I did about two months later. If I hadn't been pregnant, I
wouldn't have married Dice, but since I was, I married him for the
sake of the baby.

(DICE *enters.*)

DICE: Woman, don't you do nothing else but write in that diary?

EBONY: Oh, I'm sorry, I'll put it away.

DICE: No! Don't put it away just because I said so. My God, don't
you have a mind of your own?

EBONY: Then I won't put it away. I'll do whatever you want me to
do.

DICE: I want you to do whatever you want to do, that's what I
want.

EBONY: Okay.

DICE: You sure aren't the type of girl I thought you were. I thought
you had your head on straight.

EBONY: I'm sorry.

(DICE *backslaps her, and* EBONY *cries.*)

DICE: Stop it! Stop saying you're sorry for everything. Why don't you tell me off and do what you want to do? *(There's a knock at the door.)* Get the door.

(LINDA *enters. She looks at* DICE *but doesn't say anything to him.*)

LINDA: Yoo-hoo! Ebony, dear.

(EBONY *tries to hide her face and sound happy.*)

EBONY: Hi, Ma!

LINDA: Hi. Look at what I picked out for the baby. Isn't it cute?

EBONY: Yeah, it's nice, Ma.

DICE: Hey, Moms, why don't you teach Ebony how to shop for a kid?

(LINDA *gives* DICE *a look of disgust, then looks at* EBONY.)

LINDA: What's wrong, Ebony?

EBONY: Nothing. Just a little morning sickness, I guess.

LINDA *(slightly laughing):* It's three o'clock in the afternoon. Don't you think it's a little late to get sick now? Ha, ha. *(A tear runs down* EBONY's *eye.)* Hey, Ebony, you really are sick, huh?

DICE: Yeah, Moms, that's all she does around here is write in that diary of hers and get sick all the time. I wish somebody would do something with her. She's getting to be disgusting.

LINDA: Look, first of all, I'm not your moms. Second, you're the last person to start talking about disgusting, okay?

DICE: Look, old lady, you are in my house. If you don't like the way I talk, get out!

LINDA: You bastard, what makes you—

EBONY *(cutting in):* Mom, leave it alone, he didn't mean that.

DICE: Who says I didn't mean it? This old hag is gonna come in my house and insult me? Naw, it ain't gonna be like that. I'm gonna get me a beer in the kitchen, and when I come back, I want you out of here. (DICE *exits.*)

LINDA: The nerve of that bastard. I don't know how you put up with him.

EBONY: Mom, I know he's not the greatest but he's not all that bad. And he is the father of my baby. Anyway, I don't want to talk about it. I don't feel well.

LINDA: Oh, let me help you to the sofa. You should lay down for a while. (LINDA *tries to support* EBONY *by grabbing hold of* EBONY's *arms.*)

EBONY: Ouch!

LINDA: What's wrong? *(She looks at* EBONY's *arm.) Oh, my God, what happened?*

(BRENDA, LISA, *and* DAD *enter. They are only seen by* EBONY, *who becomes very confused.*)

BRENDA: Ebony! I suppose you're gonna tell her it was all Dice's fault?

EBONY *(to* BRENDA*):* No, I'm not! *(To* LINDA*:)* Mom, I burned myself with the iron.

(LINDA *examines the mark on* EBONY's *arm.*)

LINDA: Yeah, this is an iron mark, but how did you burn yourself this high and this hard?

BRENDA: Yeah, Ebony, how'd you do that? You gonna blame it all on Dice now?

LISA: Yeah, gonna blame it on him now?

EBONY: Mom, I don't know, it just happened. I don't want to talk about it.

LINDA: Dice did it, didn't he?

(EBONY *doesn't say anything.*)

BRENDA: Well, Ebony, who did it?

LISA: Who did it, Ebony?

DAD: Ebony, you can tell me the truth.

LINDA: Ebony, tell me how you got the burn now!

BRENDA: Go ahead and tell her.

LINDA: This is the last time I'm going to ask you.

EBONY *(yelling):* Yes, he did it!

BRENDA: I knew you were gonna blame it on him. What did you do to provoke him?

LISA: Yeah, what did *you* do, Ebony?

DAD: Did you provoke him, Ebony?

(EBONY *looks at them all.*)

EBONY: Nothing! I didn't do anything. He was drunk.

BRENDA: You expect me to believe that? You didn't cook that night, isn't that why he burned you?

DAD: Is that why, Princess?

(EBONY *looks at her father.*)

EBONY: No, Daddy!

LINDA: Ebony, who are you talking to? Don't try to get off the subject.

BRENDA: *Don't* get off the subject, Ebony.

LISA: Don't even try it.

DAD: Getting off the subject isn't the way out. Tell the truth.

LISA: She can't tell the truth. She's evil.

LINDA: Ebony, I want to know why you stay here and put up with this. Why do you stay with him?

EBONY *(crying):* Because of the baby.

BRENDA: Always putting it on someone else. You're never the cause of anything, huh?

LISA: Huh, Ebony?

DAD: Is this true, Ebony?

BRENDA: Answer him, Ebony.

EBONY *(looking at her father):* It is for the baby. I don't love Dice.

(LINDA *looks at* EBONY *and realizes that* EBONY *believes someone else is there.* LINDA *stands back and watches.)*

BRENDA: You married Dice for his money, didn't you? You probably *wanted* to get pregnant so you'd be sure to hook him.

LISA: What a sneaky way to hook a man. Yep! That's what you done.

EBONY: I don't care about the money! It's the baby—so he'll have a nice home.

BRENDA: And at the same time you have a nice home too. What a coincidence.

DAD: Come on, you can tell Daddy the truth. Is that why, Princess? Smart thinking, if you ask me.

BRENDA: Stop playing stupid, Ebony. You'll put up with anything to get to his money.

EBONY: No!

LISA: Yes, you *would*. You're evil.

DAD: Tell Daddy the truth. Don't you trust me?

EBONY: I trust you, Daddy, but money isn't why.

DAD: You just don't love me anymore. *(Exits.)*

EBONY: Yes, I do, Daddy. I wish I could tell you. Come back so I can tell you, Daddy, I do love you. I love you more now than ever before.

BRENDA: You shouldn't have lied to him.

LISA *(laughing):* But she can't tell the truth.

(EBONY *falls on her knees and starts to hit the floor.)*

EBONY *(yelling):* I'm not lying. I'm not.

(EBONY's *tantrum continues until her mother slaps her.* BRENDA *and* LISA *exit as* EBONY *comes out of it.* LINDA *hugs* EBONY.)

LINDA: Stop! Stop doing this to yourself. All these years and I didn't know how much you missed him. I'm sorry, Ebony.

EBONY *(crying to her mother):* It is for the baby.

LINDA: The *baby!* Do you even want to have the baby? Do you want to bring a child into this nightmare?

(DICE *enters with a beer in his hand.*)

DICE: Of course she does. That's gonna be my son, right, Ebony?

LINDA *(sarcastic):* And what if it's a girl? Are you gonna kill it?

DICE: Naw, I'll probably sell it and try again. *(He laughs.)* Anyway, aren't you supposed to be out of my house?

EBONY: Mom, please don't start again. Just go. I'll call you later.

LINDA: I'm not leaving without you. Come with me. You can leave him now.

DICE: *Get* out, old lady.

(DICE *pushes* LINDA.)

LINDA *(reaching out to* EBONY): Ebony, come on.

DICE *(yelling):* Get out!

LINDA *(pleading):* Ebony, please.

(EBONY *ignores her mother and lies down on the couch.*)

DICE: You see? She doesn't want to go. Now get out!

(LINDA *looks at* EBONY, *who does not respond.* LINDA *puts her head down, gets her things, and lays the gift for the baby beside* EBONY.)

LINDA: God be with you, Ebony.

(LINDA *exits.* DICE *slams the door after her.*)

DICE: I don't want that witch over here again, you hear that? (EBONY *doesn't say anything. She starts to hum.*) Do you hear that, girl?

(EBONY *stops humming.*)

EBONY: Yeah. I hear.

(DICE *notices* EBONY's *tears. He looks at her with a little bit of care.*)

DICE: It ain't that bad, is it?

EBONY: What?

DICE: You and me. We ain't that bad off, are we . . . ? Naw, you don't get to crying till your mother start coming over, filling your head about leaving me. (DICE *puts his hands on her face.*) You ain't never gonna leave me, huh? (*He takes his hands and shakes her head no for her.*) Naw, you ain't gonna never leave me. We got a baby to raise. Hey! Maybe we should move somewhere far away. By ourselves. Hey, you like that idea? (DICE *shakes* EBONY's *head yes.*) Yeah, that's what we're gonna have to do. To get away from your momma. (DICE *gulps down the rest of his beer and crushes the can in his hand. He moves away from* EBONY.) Yep, that's what we're gonna have to do.

(DICE *exits into the kitchen, deep in thought.* EBONY *lies there for a while then raises up and looks after him.*)

EBONY: No, Dice, I ain't never gonna leave you . . . (*pause*) . . . for our baby.

(EBONY *looks at her stomach and rubs it, rocking herself and singing a lullaby to the baby. While she sings, the lights find the* YOUNG EBONY *in the past in* EBONY's *old bedroom. The* YOUNG EBONY *is playing with her doll. Somewhere behind the* YOUNG EBONY, *in another room, her parents can be heard arguing. The* YOUNG EBONY *begins singing the same lullaby to her doll. After a while the older* EBONY *starts to hum the lullaby while* YOUNG EBONY *talks to her doll. The older* EBONY *doesn't relate to this past scene at all. She continues to hum almost as though she were ignoring this memory of a little girl's fantasy for the future.*)

YOUNG EBONY (*rocking her doll*): Dolly, when I grow up, I ain't gonna be like my Mommy and Daddy, always fighting. And when you're in your room, you won't hear any arguing, 'cause I'm gonna find me a good man that treats me special. He's gonna be smart and he's gonna love me and you a whole lot. Okay, dolly? *(She smiles at the doll.)* I love you, dolly. My little baby doll.

(She gets up and closes the bedroom door, shutting out the arguing. She sits again, rocking her doll. She yawns, and the older EBONY *does also.)*

YOUNG EBONY *(looking at her doll):* Hey, you're getting sleepy, huh? And I haven't even fed you yet.

(YOUNG EBONY sighs and hums the lullaby with the older EBONY *as the lights slowly fade to black.)*

PAMELA MARIVA MSHANA

I was born in Pomona, California, and grew up in the Los Angeles area. Since the 1987 Young Playwrights Festival, I have been attending New York University as a dramatic-writing major. I have also had two plays that were finalists in the California Young Playwrights Festivals. In August 1988 I went to Sydney, Australia, for three weeks to see *Ebony* produced as a finalist in the International Young Playwrights Festival, which was sponsored by the Seymour Center (Youth Theater) and the Sydney Opera House.

These experiences allowed me to see my play *Ebony* both workshopped and produced. I will have my play *A Toast to Leslie* produced at the Gaslamp Quarter Theater in San Diego in January 1989. Along with these things I am presently working on a short documentary film. This is my first film project, and it is serving as a great learning tool as I continue to expand my screenwriting ability.

My future goals include graduating from New York University and then pursuing a writing career.

ABOUT THE PLAY

In a couple of cases it has been said that *Ebony* is a play about a black family that repeats mistakes over generations. People making comments such as this agree that the dialogue suggests a black family. I feel that this is not necessarily true, because the way my characters speak is the way a particular class of people speaks. It is not a racial distinction, it is a social-class distinction. I would like to set the record straight by saying that although *Ebony* is usually cast black, I am not making a statement that this situation only happens in black families. I feel that the theme is universally true for all races.

SPARKS IN THE PARK

by Noble Mason Smith
(age eighteen when play was written)
Yakima, Washington

NOTE:
For the purpose of publication in this collection, certain words have been changed by the playwright, and some profanity has been deleted from the working script of the play as performed at Playwrights Horizons, New York City, September 15 through October 11, 1987.

Sparks in the Park was first performed at Playwrights Horizons on September 15, 1987. The director was Gary Pearle. Playwright adviser was Alfred Uhry. The cast:

BARRY DANIELS	Todd Merrill
BEN ECKERT	Doug Hutchison
STEPHANIE ECKERT	Cynthia Nixon
LOUIS REYNOLDS, CHUCK HOLLISTER	John Vennema
JANICE ENGLISH, BARRY'S MOM	Nancy Giles
INDIAN WAITER, BUDDY HOLLISTER, FRENCH WAITER, BART	Oliver Platt
AGENT 4-H, DR. RUDOLPH SCHMEER, CRAIG STRONGMAN, GUY RICHMONT	Stephen Mellor
DR. RENEE SCHMEER	Susan Greenhill

SCENE 1:
The Zim Zam Café—Bombay, India.
Barry's room.
Dr. Schmeer's office.

SCENE 2:
The park.

SCENE 3:
A café in France.
Barry's room.
Normandy castle.

SCENE 4:
The park.

For Dinky and Dad
And special thanks to—

Gary Pearle, Nancy Quinn, and everyone at the Young Playwrights Festival. Andre Bishop and the crew at Playwrights Horizons. The incredible New York cast. Alfred and Jolly.

And . . . Kendra.

SCENE ONE

The Zim Zam Café, a seedy little dive off Queen Victoria Street, Bombay, India. Center stage is a small, dilapidated table with two chairs. A MAN, tan shirt, ascot, and pith helmet, sits at another table, up right. He is reading a book and smoking a pipe. The room is illuminated by a single, exposed bulb. Christmas tree lights surround various religious posters and plaster deities. Outside, the sounds and voices of the city can be overheard: The whiny whistle of a pipe and the tinny beat of a drum play dully on the street. Car horns honk constantly, followed by shouts of anger. A MAN selling his wares comes closer, then fades into the oblivion of voices.

A WOMAN enters the room. She is dressed like a tourist; dumpy clothes, straw hat perched upon her head. She walks hesitantly up to the table at center stage and looks around nervously. Her eyes come to rest on the filthy table and the sticky chair. From her shoulder bag she takes out a butt-protection sheet and sets it on the chair. She maneuvers herself over the chair and plops down carefully, as if sitting on a toilet.

An INDIAN WAITER, wearing Punjabi pants and a long collarless white shirt, comes up to the table. The woman does not notice him. She is reading the menu, running her finger down the list of confusing names. The waiter becomes impatient. He scratches his butt. He glances at the man in the corner. He peeps at his watch. He taps his pencil on his notepad. The WOMAN takes off her hat. The WAITER looks at the top of her head. Suddenly he smacks her head with his notepad.

WAITER: *(His voice thick with accent. He shouts.)* Big Scary Bug! *(The WOMAN jumps and lets out a little gasp.)* Whad wood you luk?

JANICE: *(She is American. Her voice is typical West Coast. She looks up and points to an item on the menu.)* I would like the cantaloupe and—

WAITER *(interrupting):* Whad do you say?

JANICE: Cantaloupe. *(She holds her hands in a ball shape.)*

WAITER: *(Shaking his head from side to side, he yells offstage.)* Salim! Kandy Loop?

OFFSTAGE VOICE: No!

WAITER: *(Beat. Bellowing.)* Out of seazun!

JANICE *(pointing to another item):* All right. What about the dahl and rice with chutney—

WAITER: *(Starts to write.)* One dahl and rice with . . . *(He stops, a frustrated look on his face.)* Oh, pleaze! Dat is onely on da dinna menu. *(He crosses his arms, purses his lips, and wags his head even faster.)*

JANICE *(becoming impatient):* Okay. How about oatmeal?

WAITER *(throwing up his arms):* Ahhh. . . . Dat iz brakefast!

JANICE *(upset):* Well, how am I supposed to tell. They are all mixed up. *(Pause.)* Just give me an orange juice.

WAITER: *(Sighs, turns to exit stage left.)* One cheeze sandawich— *(He says with relief, not quite understanding the order.)*

JANICE *(with bewilderment):* What!? No. I said one orange juice!

WAITER: *(An equally puzzled look. He repeats himself.)* One cheeze sandawich. *(JANICE holds up a hand and gestures for the WAITER to read her lips. JANICE and the WAITER at the same time:)*

JANICE: Orrr-annn-juice!

WAITER: Orrr-annn-cheeze sandawich! *(JANICE screams and jumps up. The MAN in the pith helmet crosses down to the table.)*

LOUIS *(in a prim British accent):* Excuse me. May I be of some assistance?

JANICE *(slumping down in her chair):* Oh, good. You speak the language?

LOUIS *(to the* WAITER*):* Ravi.

WAITER: Yes, Mister Loowy?

LOUIS: The mem-sahib would like one or-dranz-goozie. *(He says the word putting stresses on consonants, stretching vowels, until it sounds like a completely "foreign" word.)*

WAITER: *(Raises his eyebrows.)* Well, if she wanted one or-dranz-goozie, why did she not just ask for one!? *(He sulks off, muttering under his breath.)* Stupid American cow . . .

JANICE: I can't seem to say anything they understand. Hindu English is like . . .

LOUIS *(continuing her sentence):* Like a completely different language. Yes, I know all too well. *(He stares at something on the floor.)* It's slurred and mixed up and jumbled about. *(He stomps on a bug.)* Quite annoying, really. *(Pause.)* Oftentimes it's like . . . talking to an American.

JANICE *(peeved):* Thank you.

LOUIS: *(Sits down.)* I'm only kidding of course. *(Snickering at his little joke.)* My name is Reynolds, Louis Reynolds.

JANICE: Mine's English, Janice English.

LOUIS: Oh, English! How delightful. *(Pause.)* Quite a dismal city, you know. Sometimes I feel as if I were going mad myself.

(From up right, a MAN dressed in a dark "G-Man" suit and sunglasses enters and crosses to the table up right, unnoticed by JANICE or LOUIS.)

JANICE: Yes, I know the feeling. *(Pause.)* So, what do you do here in Bombay, Louis?

LOUIS: I work at the embassy, British, that is. If you think it is trouble ordering orange juice, try making them understand the procedure for granting a Pakistani visa. Why, once—

JANICE: *(She notices the STRANGER, who is standing staring intently at her. She interrupts LOUIS and grabs his arm.)* Louis! *(She leans forward. He stops and stares at her curiously.)* Louis. Do you see that man standing over there? *(She points to the corner.)*

LOUIS *(staring at her):* Excuse me?

JANICE: Listen to me. There is a man standing in the corner. Pretend to wipe your forehead on your sleeve or something. (LOUIS *shrinks back, stares at JANICE, then pretends to wipe his forehead on his sleeve, still staring at her.)* No . . . no. Pretend to sniff under your arm or something, then take a peek at the man.

LOUIS: *(His eyes grow wider.)* Oh, I see . . . a trick! *(He fingers his nose. Then, he slowly, awkwardly sniffs under his arm and glances under his shoulder at the man. He turns back around with an excited look.)* Oh, my! I do believe that man was watching me.

JANICE: *(Grabs his arm, pulling him close.)* Listen, Louis. I have to tell you something. A dangerous secret . . . about me.

LOUIS: Yes . . . yes . . . do tell.

JANICE: *(Fumbles with her sunglasses and puts them on. She takes a deep breath.)* Louis . . . I'm a spy!

LOUIS: *(A long pause as he leans back, then laughs aloud.)* Ripping! Absolutely ripping.

JANICE *(growing impatient):* Listen to me. I really am a spy.

LOUIS: How delightful. A prankster like myself.

JANICE *(extremely serious):* I have a gun in my purse!

LOUIS: *(Stops snickering, leans toward her.)* A what?

JANICE: A gun! *(She thrusts her bag under the table and opens it for him.)*

LOUIS: My God. What are you doing here? What in God's name is a spy doing in Bombay?

JANICE: Actually, I'm just passing through. My plane was shot down over the Himalayas . . . my pilot killed. I've spent the last month trying to get to Tibet. I was supposed to meet a contact here—

LOUIS: *(Shudders with excitement.)* And you think that man over there is—

JANICE: Either my contact or an agent sent to kill me. He has trailed me since I left the hotel.

(The MAN walks over to the table. JANICE and LOUIS sit completely still.)

MAN: Good afternoon, miss. *(He pulls on one of his earlobes.)*

JANICE: Good afternoon.

MAN: I don't mean to intrude . . . *(He jerks his head to the left.)* but I overheard you asking for some orange juice . . . *(He puts both hands under his chin and wiggles his fingers.)*

JANICE: Yes . . . *(She sticks out her tongue and touches her nose.)* orange juice would be nice for this climate . . . *(She pulls back her coat and squeezes one of her breasts.)* Would you enjoy a cigarette? *(Holds out a pack.)*

MAN: Dunhills. . . . *(He stresses the Dun part.)* My favorite. Would you enjoy a breath mint . . . a Certs perhaps? *(Holds out a pack.)*

JANICE: *(Sighs.)* Cert-ainly . . . *(She says, completing the code.)*

MAN: *(Sits down, wipes his forehead.)* I am Agent Four-H. I have been trying to find you for the past three days— *(He stares at* LOUIS.*)*

JANICE *(to 4-H):* He's okay.

AGENT 4-H: *(Nods.)* Do you have the plans?

(Unseen, the WAITER *comes onstage holding a small tray covered with a napkin.)*

JANICE: Yes, I have them . . .

WAITER: *(He stops.)* Here is your— *(He pulls off the napkin. On the tray is a German Luger.)* Cheeze sandawich! *(He takes the gun and points it at* JANICE.*)*

LOUIS: Oh, my God. . . . He's got a *gun!*

(Suddenly JANICE *swings her purse and knocks the* WAITER *into a spin.* 4-H *lunges across the table, flipping the cigarettes he's been holding into the* WAITER's *face. The* WAITER *jumps on a chair.* 4-H *grabs his arm. The gun swings back and forth.* JANICE *and* LOUIS *hold on to each other, screaming. The gun is pointed at the ceiling. A shot is fired. Blackness. Music erupts as the stage is cleared. A special light comes up on a* YOUNG MAN, *who appears downstage out of nowhere. He stares at the audience.)*

BARRY: Aren't plays amazing? I think I love writing more than anything in the world. You sit down at a typewriter, stare at that empty, white page . . . and pretty soon . . . voices start talking in your head.

(Voices offstage.)

WAITER: Now I have you and I'm not going to let you go.

JANICE *(screaming):* Loooouuuuuiiiisss!

AGENT 4-H: Don't move, waiter . . . or your ass is chutney.

LOUIS: Oh MY!

BARRY *(listening):* Amazing! Once they get started, they just don't stop.

(Voices offstage.)

JANICE: The doooooor!

LOUIS: Whooaoaooaoa.

WAITER: I've got a hold on you!

LOUIS: Those are my privvies you're groping.

WAITER: I thought dey were da kandy loops.

AGENT 4-H: Outta season, pal!

BARRY: There is one thing I don't like about writing, though. I don't like it when I write something that I think is really great *(pause)* and my best friend thinks it's stupid.

(Lights up. We are now in BARRY's room. A futon chair sits stage right. A desk and bookshelf are up center. A small wastebasket is placed next to the desk. Sitting on the chair in front of the desk is STEPH. BARRY stares at her. She stares back.)

BARRY *(softly):* What do you mean, "plot manipulation?"

STEPH: Well . . . I mean . . . *(She chooses her words carefully.)* it was okay, kind of funny almost . . . until . . . it turned out that . . . ummm . . . Louis Reynolds was a double agent working for the KGB, and that he just happened to have that private jet on that . . . island or whatever.

BARRY: He didn't just happen to have it there. It was all planned out by the Taoist Terrorists!

STEPH: But you didn't explain that!

BARRY: Well . . . it was obvious. *(Pause.)* Wasn't it?

STEPH *(looking away):* No.

BARRY: Hey, I didn't ask you over here to criticize my play to little shreds.

STEPH: It was lame. What am I supposed to say? *(He doesn't answer.)* I think I'd better go. *(She gets up.)*

BARRY: No . . . stay. You're right. It's worthless trash.

STEPH: Well, for comedy adventure, it was pretty good.

BARRY: No . . . no. *(Slumps his shoulders.)* My fate is incurable. I'm destined to be an insurance agent like my father.

STEPH *(angry):* Don't you ever say that again.

BARRY: Listen, Steph, I'm serious. I cannot write anymore. I'm a literary loser. I used to put out some great stuff, but now . . . *(raspberry)*

STEPH: Don't be pretentious.

BARRY: *(Repeats the word.)* Pretentious.

STEPH: Barry, you are one of the most *(pause)* talented guys I know. But your best stuff comes when you don't try so hard. Your poems are some of the most beautiful things I have ever—

BARRY *(interrupting):* POEMS! Po-ems. Poems are for weenies. I want to write something that people will go to and cry and laugh at. I want to sit in the back row of my play and watch real live people live my words. Poems are hollow. I can't explain.

STEPH: Look. People know when a writer is lying. Tell about something you know. Write about something true.

BARRY: You want true! Watch *Wild Kingdom*. This is the Theater.

STEPH: But you have so much in your life—

BARRY *(cutting her off):* I have nothing. I'm boring. This world is boring. My room is boring. *(Pause.)* And you are boring.

STEPH: I'm leaving.

BARRY *(screaming):* I CANNOT TAKE IT ANYMORE!!!

MOM: *(Offstage. She has a loud, ear-splitting voice.)* Barry! Barry, what are you doing?

BARRY: *(Moans.)* Nothing, Mom.

MOM *(offstage):* Listen, Barry . . . are you writing plays again? I thought I told you not to write anymore. If you can't write without screaming every five minutes, I don't want you doing this at all. You are giving me an ulcer.

BARRY: Okay.

MOM *(offstage):* Barry? What did you say?

BARRY: All right. God . . . give me a break. *(Pause, then to the audience:)* I really think I'm going insane. Do you want to know why I'm going insane? Well, I'll tell you anyway. *(He pulls off a poster that is tacked to his bookcase.)* It's all because of this. *(Holds it up for the audience to see.)* Can you read it? It says, "Write a play and see it produced by top professionals in New York City in America's Annual Young Playwrights Festival." Pretty neat. My English teacher gave it to me just before school was out for the summer. *(Beat.)* Just the kind of thing an English teacher would give you right before summer. This thing has been like a curse. It's killing me. Don't get me wrong. It's not like I have to do this or anything. It's just become like a quest. I always thought . . . hey, I could write a play. I mean . . . listen. I have been to so many bad plays in my life. Stupid, idiotic plays . . . plays that make you say, "My God, what kind of madman wrote this?" And do you know why there are so many bad plays? *(Yells:)* BECAUSE THEY ARE IMPOSSIBLE TO WRITE! *(Pause, waiting for his MOTHER's voice.)* I have been sitting in this stupid room all month. It's not that I don't have anything to say. That's just it. I have too much to say. I'm too incredibly smart. Write a play . . . write a play. *(Pause.)* Have you ever gone to a play and sat through about the first ten minutes, maybe even up to intermission, without having any idea what was going on? People are sitting around you, laughing, or crying their brains out, and you're just sitting there thinking, "God, my tongue hurts." *(Beat.)* What's worse is when you go to a play, one you really like, and they give it this completely moronic ending. I hate them. I have decided that I hate plays more than anything in the world. That's it. I give up. *(He sits down on the futon couch.)* No more plays for me. *(He leans back.)* Hey . . . what's this? *(He reaches behind his back and pulls out a rolled-up script. Inside is a toy helicopter.* BARRY *takes out the helicopter, unrolls the script, and stares at it. Recognition comes into his face.)* Hey . . . this is one of my best works. *(Flips the pages.)* The Karma Cowboy. *(Pause.)* Great name, isn't it? *(Sits on the edge of the couch.)* It's all about this guy, Buddy Hollister, who flew helicopter gun ships in Vietnam. *(He turns a page.)* Ahhh . . . here it is, scene three. Vienna, Austria. A creepy mental institution.

(As BARRY *is speaking, the lights dim. Weird string music plays. A bust of Freud appears from stage left and rolls across the stage behind the scrim and stops. A special comes up on* BARRY.)

BARRY: Buddy's been locked up 'cause everyone thinks he's insane. When the curtain comes up, Chuck, Buddy's older brother, is coming to visit him for the first time . . . all the way from El Paso.

*(*BARRY *looks at the script. From stage right,* CHUCK *enters. He is wearing cowboy boots, a cowboy hat, old Wrangler jeans, a beat-up corduroy jacket, and a bolo tie. He looks around the stage and stops by the desk. He takes off his hat and sets it down.)*

BARRY *(flipping through the papers):* Uhhh . . . Chuck is nervous. He is tired and worn out from the flight. Every so often he looks about the room. He glances at the door in anticipation.

*(*CHUCK, *following* BARRY's *directions, glances about the room.)*

BARRY: Chuck reaches into his pocket and . . .

(CHUCK *reaches into his pocket—*)

BARRY: He reaches for a . . .

(CHUCK *fumbles in his pockets for some time. Finally he looks at* BARRY *and opens his mouth as if to speak.*)

BARRY: For a . . . *(Flips a page.)* For a gun!

(CHUCK *shakes his head, then starts to pull a Colt .45 from his jacket.*)

BARRY: No, wait. Not a gun . . . a pack of cigarettes.

(CHUCK *rolls his eyes, puts the gun back, and pulls out a pack of cigarettes.*)

BARRY: They are Dunhills.

CHUCK: *(Squints at* BARRY.) Now hold it right there, you little—

BARRY: No, wait! They are Marlboros.

CHUCK: That's betta. *(He puts one in his mouth. From another pocket,* CHUCK *takes out a huge box of wooden kitchen matches.*)

BARRY: Chuck lights the match—

(CHUCK *lights the match with his thumb.*)

BARRY *(reading the script):* —on his shoe.

(CHUCK *sighs, blows out the match, and lights another one off the bottom of his shoe.*)

BARRY *(looking up):* Marlboros. The real man's cigarette.

CHUCK: You said it.

BARRY: Okay . . . ummmmm. *(Pause.)* Suddenly from the hallway come several screams.

(We hear several weak, toneless utterances.)

BARRY *(upset):* They are creepy, demented screams. . . . Obviously the utterances of deranged individuals. (BARRY *lets forth a deranged scream. The offstage voices match his intensity.)*

CHUCK: My God . . . what in the Holy Moses . . . where in the hay-eck . . . (CHUCK *stops as a particularly strange laugh erupts stage right.)*

(DR. RUDOLPH SCHMEER, *deranged psychiatrist, enters the room backward, talking to someone offstage.)*

SCHMEER: —and den, zee strudel fell on his lap and he screamed, "Oh, my . . . last time it was banana cake!" *(Offstage voices laugh.)*

CHUCK: *(He takes a step toward* SCHMEER.) Hello, Dr. Uhhh—

SCHMEER: *(Whirls around and stares wide-eyed, looking* CHUCK *up and down.)* Dr. Schmeer, Dr. Rudolph Schmeer—

(OFFSTAGE VOICES, *everyone at the same time, building to a hysterical crescendo:)*

VOICE ONE: Crying in a demented fashion.

VOICE TWO: Repeating, "Schmeer, Schmeer, Rudolph Schmeer . . ."

VOICE THREE: Laughter, strange and twisted.

VOICE FOUR. Repeating, "Who is it? Who is that? Who is it? What is he doing . . ."

SCHMEER *(raising his voice until the last word,* clinic): I am in charge of THIS CLINIC!! (The voices stop. He stares at CHUCK.) And you must be?

CHUCK: I'm Chuck Hollister from El Paso, Texas. *(He reaches out his hand to shake* SCHMEER's. SCHMEER *looks disdainfully at*

CHUCK's *hand, and daintily touches* CHUCK's *fingers in a half hand-shake.)*

SCHMEER: Ahhhh . . . Tex-ass. *(Motions for* CHUCK *to sit on the futon couch.* BARRY *gets up and moves to the box, down right.)* Texas is a very beautiful place, Meester Hole-ister . . . quite luffly . . . rolling-ga heels . . . very attractive cowz unt sheeps. *(Sneering.)* But it's a long way from Owstria now, isn't it!?

CHUCK: Well, uhhhh . . .

SCHMEER: So. What do you think of our little country, Meester Hole-ister?

CHUCK: Uhhh . . . well, I haven't had much time to look around much. But I mean . . . it's nice and all—

SCHMEER: Nice, only nice!? *(His words are biting.)*

CHUCK *(taken aback):* Uhhh . . . well, real nice.

SCHMEER: Real nice. . . . *(He stares at* CHUCK.*)* I would say it iz beautiful, Meester Hole-ister, the most beautiful place in the world perhaps *(pause, then with contempt),* probably even more beautiful than El Paso!

CHUCK *(standing up):* Now what are you gettin at?

SCHMEER: What am I getting at, Meester Hole-ister . . . what I am getting at iz that I don't think you know what you are doing here. I don't think you know, using a Tex-ass fa-raize, your ass from axle grease!

CHUCK: Listen, Schmoo—

SCHMEER *(screaming):* SCHMEER!

CHUCK: Whatever. *(Crosses to* SCHMEER.*)* I think I know what you're tryin' ta do. I may be just a dumb shikticker from Texas, but no fancy high-tootin' doctor is goin' ta tell me what ta do. I know why I'm here. I'm here ta git my little brother . . . Buddy!

SCHMEER: *(Completely changing his attitude. He smiles meekly.)*
You must know that Butty is a fairy *(pause)* zick man.

CHUCK: I know, but—

SCHMEER: He has one of the worst kisses *(beat)* of schizophrenic
sarcosis I have ever vitnessed.

CHUCK: Well, where I come from, out on the range and all, you can
be pretty weird and get away with it. Sometimes it's all a man has
ta do ta pass the time. Why, I remember this one time, we took this
sheep and three gallons of halla-pana peppers an—

SCHMEER *(interrupting):* Listen to me!

CHUCK: I'm a-listanen.

SCHMEER: Your brother was shot down over the Chang Mai Penin-
sula in 1973. He says he was rescued by a Chinese fisherman. He
shpent the last nine years with this man shtudying the ways of Toy-
ism.

CHUCK: My Gawd! I didn't imagine it was that awful.

SCHMEER: Oh . . . yes . . . it get vorse. We have reason to believe he is lying. We believe that he was brain-vashed by the Red
Army, forced to shmuggle weapons back and forth between Thai-
land, captured by communist agents, and then eshcaped through
East Berlin—

CHUCK: How do you know all this?

SCHMEER: It's just a hunch *(beat)*, but I know he's lying. He has
this crazy fantasy that this Chinese man found him, took him to
live in this Shangra-la-la land, then sent him back to shpread this
massage of eternal piss.

CHUCK *(overcome with grief): Oh, my Gawd!* I never knew he
could've become so twisted. The poor little sonofaseabiscuit!

SCHMEER: Yes, it is quite sad, I know.

(Lights suddenly go out. A special comes up on BARRY. CHUCK *and* SCHMEER *freeze in their positions—*CHUCK *sobbing with hands covering his head,* SCHMEER *looking forlornly toward the audience.)*

BARRY *(to audience):* God . . . this is beautiful. Wait a minute. How about a little love interest, though? *(Pencils in on his script.)* This is beautiful. *(A slender* WOMAN *dressed exactly like* SCHMEER *comes onstage and walks up behind* SCHMEER. *She taps him on the shoulder. He hands her the clipboard. She takes his place.)* That's the thrill of being an author . . . total control, I love it.

(Lights out on BARRY. *Lights back up on the new* SCHMEER *and* CHUCK.*)*

CHUCK *(not looking up):* Oh, Doctor. What in the world am I gonna do?

BARRY *(pointing to the ceiling):* Red gel.

(A steamy red gel appears over CHUCK*'s head. Slinky lounge music plays. The new* SCHMEER *pulls a barrette from her hair, which falls into a cascading mane about her shoulders. She takes off her lab coat and drops it on the floor. She is clad in a sexy red nightie. She removes her glasses . . . walks over and stands behind* CHUCK, *massaging his shoulders.)*

CHUCK *(head down):* Oh, Doctor. I feel like my guts are dying inside. Like a dull knife is diggin' into my very innards. I feel all hot and cold, like the mist that rises off the desert in the early mornin'—blood red, deep and yearning like the sky was on *fire.*

(He looks up at her, surprised by her sudden change. She straddles him. They kiss madly. Suddenly, BUDDY *steps onstage. The music stops. The lights come on.* CHUCK *pulls away from* SCHMEER *and stares in disbelief.)*

CHUCK: Oh, my God! It's Buddy.

*(*BUDDY *walks up to the desk. He is wearing cowboy pajamas and has a white Ace bandage wrapped around his head. He looks at the two in bewilderment. In one hand he holds a Japanese geisha doll.)*

BUDDY *(with Texas drawl):* Chang dow? *(Pause as he stares at the two.)* Dee oo may? *(Pause.)* Chu . . . chy . . . ch . . . *(*CHUCK *spits in the palm of his hand, slaps his thigh, and points his hand in the shape of a gun at* BUDDY. BUDDY *immediately recognizes the old "hello" sign.* BUDDY *drops the doll into the wastebasket. His voice cracks with sudden realization.)* Chucky! It is you. *(*CHUCK *rushes forward to hug* BUDDY. *At the last moment,* BUDDY *brings his hands together in the traditional Oriental sign of namaste, poking* CHUCK *in the neck.* CHUCK *glances at* SCHMEER. *He licks his lips, then punches* BUDDY *playfully in the shoulder.)*

CHUCK: It's been too darn long, little brother!

BUDDY *(shaking his head):* Ahhh, Chuck. I've missed ya, man. I never stopped thinking about you and Ma, not once, no sir—

CHUCK: I just can't believe it, pal. You look great. A little pale maybe, but that desert sun will tan your hide in no time!

BUDDY *(somber, dropping his head):* Chuck, I have to tell you something.

CHUCK: Yeah, what is it, little brother?

(Both men stare at SCHMEER. *She nods encouragement for* BUDDY *to continue.)*

BUDDY: I can't go back with you.

CHUCK: *(Looks from* BUDDY *to* SCHMEER *with a frantic smile on his lips.)* What do ya mean? You look fine. I expected ta find ya with your head shaved and lectrodes stickin' out of your brain and all, and rantin' in a room with pillows all over the wall, but you're doin' just fine!

BUDDY *(putting a hand to the side of his head):* It's not that, Chuck, I'm a different man now. A lot has happened to me over the years . . . a lot I can't explain.

CHUCK: Well, ya gotta come back, Buddy. I mean, that's partly why I'm here. It's the ranch, Buddy.

BUDDY: Yes.

CHUCK: We need ya, Buddy. You were one of the best cowhands ever in those parts, maybe even the world. The boys and me, well, we need your inspiration. We lost that special something that makes us real cowboys . . . call it guts, call it love. . . . But I need ya, Buddy, the boys need ya, Ma needs ya . . . the dog needs ya!

BUDDY: *Whiskers?!* *(Pause.)* I don't know what to say. Oh, God . . . how can I tell you this—

CHUCK: Tell me what, little brotha?

BUDDY: I'm . . . I can't . . . I can't be a cowboy no more . . .

CHUCK *(slapping BUDDY's hands):* Well, durn, boy, what do ya mean?

BUDDY: I'm . . . I mean . . . well . . . I can't . . . I can't . . . I'm a—

CHUCK: You're a what, for Chrissakes!?

SCHMEER *(screaming):* He is a VEGETARIAN!!

BUDDY *(nodding):* I'm a vegetable.

CHUCK: *(Falls to his knees.)* Jesus H. Christ. . . . *(Pause, then he looks at BARRY.)* This is the silliest durn plot I have ever heard.

BARRY: What do you mean?

CHUCK: I mean . . . as far as writing goes, you have about as much potential as a gelded calf.

SCHMEER: He iz right.

BUDDY *(in a dreamy, mellow voice):* I think you should write with honesty and love. *(He takes out a slip of paper from his shirt pocket and unfolds it.)* Your poems are some of the most beautiful—

BARRY: *(He runs up and furiously snatches the poem from* BUDDY'S *fingers.)* Give me a break. My poems are some of the cheesiest pieces of crap—

SCHMEER: No, zay are goot . . . unt do you know why?

CHUCK: Because they are honest and true, like the desert in the evening when—

BARRY *(yelling):* Shut up!

(The THREE *come up and stand several feet behind* BARRY, *encompassing him.* BARRY *looks at the script in his hand, facing the audience.* SCHMEER *puts her hand on* BARRY'S *shoulder.)*

SCHMEER *(wrapping her leg around his waist):* Young man, you have one of the vorst kisses of penile frenzy I have ever vitnessed.

CHUCK: *(Gooses him.)* That means ya need a girl.

BARRY: *(The* THREE *are practically breathing down his neck.)* AHHHHHH! Get out of my brain—

MOM *(offstage):* Barry? What are you doing?

THE THREE CHARACTERS: He's writing a play!

BARRY *(eyes wide open):* I'm writing a play. (BARRY *jumps away from the group and holds the script out in front between two hands as if he is going to rip it in half. The* CHARACTERS *cower away, shaking their heads.* BARRY *speaks resolutely.)* I am writing a play.

(He rips the script in half. BUDDY, SCHMEER, *and* CHUCK *fall dead on the floor. Blackout.)*

SCENE TWO

The park at night. Lights come up slowly. The stage is empty except for a park bench. BARRY *is sitting on the bench. He still has the ripped-up script in his hands. In the distance thunder rumbles.*

BARRY: I like thunder . . . I think. I like being outside, especially when it rains . . . just sitting. *(Pause.)* People tell you to write about what you know, but sometimes you don't even want to think about what you know. There is this room at the back of my house. It has windows all around and this high ceiling above. I'll just lay there at night . . . and the moon will be out . . . and all these creepy shadows will start swaying in the backyard. I get this desperate feeling . . . when I'm alone like that. I want to call my parents or my dog . . . or someone. But I don't. I just sit there until I start to shake and feel as if I'm going to scream.

(As he is speaking, BEN *comes onstage, unseen by* BARRY. *He is dressed in shabby skateboarder clothes. He sneaks up behind* BARRY.)

BARRY: I think I just like to scare myself. I'm pretty good at it.

*(*BEN *leans over and jabs his fingers into* BARRY'S *waist.)*

BEN *(screeching):* BEGAW! *(*BARRY *jumps.* BEN *leaps over the bench and starts to dance, singing a few lines from "Fashion" by David Bowie. Pause. He lifts his hand up, sort of waves.)* Sorry if I scared you.

BARRY: Yeah. No. It's okay.

BEN: You all right?

BARRY: Yes. I'm great.

BEN: *(Sits down next to him. Both stare at the sky.* BEN *takes out a Pez dispenser.)* Pez?

BARRY: I hate Pez.

BEN: I think it's gonna rain.

BARRY: *(Nods.)* Yes. I think it might.

BEN *(gesturing at the ripped script in* BARRY'S *hand):* What's that?

BARRY: A play. I read it to you a couple of months ago.

BEN *(naming a play):* Lacerations?

BARRY: No.

BEN: *Byzantium Revisited?*

BARRY: Nope.

BEN: *Brunch with the Devil?*

BARRY: *Breakfast with the Devil!* No, not that one either. *(Holds up the script and sighs.)* It's *The Karma Cowboy.*

BEN: Is that the one about the two gay cowpokes?

BARRY: What?

BEN: Those two guys. The one that became a Hindu and the other one— *(He stops, trying to remember.)*

BARRY: It was that memorable, huh?

BEN: I can't remember. *(Pause.)* You know, Barry, you should try writing something different for a change. You know . . . like a short story or something . . . variety.

BARRY: I don't want variety. I want to be bland and contrived, like every other writer in the world.

BEN *(leaning back, holding up his hands):* O-kay. *(Pause.)* Did you call Stephanie's house?

BARRY: Yes, but she wasn't home. *(Looks at Ben.)* Hey?

BEN: What?

BARRY: How long have her parents been like—

BEN: About to kill each other? Gosh, how long have they been married? Ten, twenty . . . twenty years.

BARRY: Why didn't they do this a long time ago?

BEN: Some people like to torture themselves. I don't really know. I really think they both love Stephanie . . . maybe that's the only reason they ever tried . . . but God . . . she's lucky she turned out as great as she did.

BARRY: Yeah!

BEN: *(Laughs.)* Yeah.

BARRY: What's so funny?

BEN: I was thinking about the day you moved into the neighborhood. I was in those bushes. *(Points.)* Right there.

BARRY: What were you doing?

BEN: I was butt-rubbing with Billy Boner.

BARRY *(laughing):* What?

BEN: In those bushes. We used to come over here every day. We'd take off all our clothes, then sort of dance around a little. *(He dances.)* Then we'd rub our butt-cheeks together. God it was fun! I can still remember the way his skin felt. He had this weird dermatitis . . . his skin was all rough . . . it felt like I was rubbing up against an elephant or something. (BEN *smiles, laughing with*

BARRY. *He loves this story. He loves telling it passionately.)* It was so . . . primal . . . you know? God, I loved that. One day I came home and my shirt was on inside out. My mom freaked. She thought I was being molested by some creep in the park. I said, "Nope, Mom . . . just Billy Boner."

BARRY: How old were you?

BEN: We must have been in the third grade. One wonderful year. Wow, I love this park. It's got something ancient about it.

BARRY: Yeah. *(The two laugh.)*

BEN *(becoming serious):* I have to ask you something. *(They try not to laugh.)* Since Billy moved away, and you're really the only friend I've got . . . will you?

BARRY *(bursting with laughter):* Butt-rub with you!? No, I don't think so.

(BEN bites BARRY's shoulder. BARRY jumps up, and BEN chases him downstage. BEN starts doing a little dance, singing a funny nonsense song, such as "Papa Oo Mau Mau" or "The Bird's the Word," joined by BARRY. They rub butt-cheeks madly. In the midst of this enters STEPHANIE. She stands for some time and stares at the two. They see her and stifle their laughter. Silence.)

BEN: Hey, I'm sorry about your mom and dad. *(Pause.)* I gotta go. *(He looks at the two awkwardly, then exits.)*

BARRY: I'm sorry, too. *(They both sit on the bench.)*

STEPH: I feel like crapola.

BARRY: It's all right, you deserve to feel like crapola.

STEPH: No, I feel worse than I ever have in my entire life.

BARRY: Your mom and dad will—

STEPH: No! They won't, thank God, they won't get back together. But it's not just that. Everything has been building for a couple of months. This just sort of finally broke me.

BARRY *(putting his arm around her shoulder):* What is it?

STEPH *(throwing up her hands):* Everything! It's everything!

BARRY: Oh, my . . . that is a problem.

STEPH: I'm serious, Barry. Sometimes I feel as if someone is squeezing my lungs, just sort of pushing all the air out of me.

BARRY: I know that feeling too.

STEPH: I really think I'm going insane sometimes.

BARRY: Everyone does.

STEPH: No, everyone doesn't. A lot of people do, but the majority doesn't.

BARRY: Have you been taking secret polls again?

STEPH: I just know. Sometimes I wish I were a little kid again. I think it was the only time when I was ever really happy.

BARRY: You mean . . . oblivious.

STEPH: Is there a difference? *(Pause.)* When I was a little kid, I remember this one time I went out in front of our house with this colored chalk. I sat down on the sidewalk and just started drawing this . . . this mural thing. I worked from like twelve noon to nine at night. When I got done, I was so proud. I ran inside and told Mom. She came out and looked at this . . . this glob of chalk thing. She said, "Uhhh . . . it's good." I was so happy. I went to bed, but I couldn't sleep. I sat by the window all night. I just kept thinking about it. I was so worried something would happen to it, like it would blow away or something. When I woke up, it was all mooshed . . . and, well, they had left the sprinklers on, and people had walked on it. It was ruined.

BARRY: Were you devastated?

STEPH: No, I forgot about it in a couple of days. I can move on to things pretty fast.

BARRY: Oh . . . not me. I'm just the opposite. When I was a little kid, I would spend hours, days on some stupid project I was making. And then I would get done, and I would look at it . . . scream and rip it up because I thought I had ruined it or something.

STEPH: I wasn't that way at all. I was such an easy kid to satisfy.

BARRY: I like to torture myself.

STEPH: That's not good. *(Pause, then blurts out:)* I always wanted a horse!

BARRY: *(Nods his head.)* I always wanted a treasure chest. I used to pray for one. I would tell God that if he gave me a treasure chest, I would use all the money to save all the poor little kids and starving animals in the world. I wanted to start this home for stray dogs and cats. All of them would come and live in this big field, and I would set up troughs and feeding bins for them. One day me and my two friends took this old wagon and went all over the neighborhood searching for strays. And you know what?

STEPH: What?

BARRY: There wasn't one single stray!

STEPH: No—

BARRY: Yes! All we found were dead ones. A dead poodle, two dead birds, and a hamster. We put them all in the wagon and set up this little cemetery in my backyard.

STEPH: That's pathetic.

BARRY: I know.

STEPH: This one Christmas Eve, I wanted to stay up until twelve sooo bad. I cried and cried to get them to let me stay up. I sat on the stairs and bawled. Finally my dad came up and sat down next to me and said, "What do you want more than anything in the world?" And of course, I said to stay up until twelve, and he said, "Okay . . . you can." I was so happy. I just sat there smiling. Then all of a sudden I jumped up and screamed, "No, wait . . . a HORSE . . . I WANT A HORSE!" and started crying all over again. *(They both laugh.)* You know, the greatest thing about being a little kid is that if something wasn't working out, you could always change it.

BARRY: Yeah . . . I guess.

STEPH: And when something you had always hoped for finally did happen, it was always a letdown.

BARRY: I don't know about that.

STEPH: *(Stares at him.)* Barry, I have this one great fear, and I can't stop thinking about it.

BARRY: What?

STEPH: You will think I'm stupid.

BARRY: No more than I already do.

STEPH: Thanks, but—

BARRY: Go ahead. I'm in a listening mood.

STEPH *(after a pause):* I'm afraid of the future . . . my future.

BARRY: What do you mean?

STEPH: I'm afraid, Barry. I'm afraid I will never be satisfied. I don't think I will ever be truly happy with anything.

BARRY: I don't think you can be happy. My God, look at the world we live in. It's demented.

STEPH: Don't you ever think about it?

BARRY: Of course, but I've sort of trained myself to realize that the greatest lesson a human being can discover is he is living in a ridiculous world, and happiness is something only found by . . . brain donors!

STEPH: Don't you think we were put on this planet for some purpose? Don't you think there is something to change?

BARRY: Yes, I think I'm here for a reason. I'm going to live my life to the fullest, but in the back of my mind this little voice will always be saying, "This isn't it."

STEPH: So—

BARRY: So . . . this is how I see it. God, or whatever, sends us to live in these bodies. We are like trees, and we have these incredible roots which tie us down. Our egos, vanities, desires—anything physical—dig into the ground, and keep us here. My goal is to pull out all those roots, one by one, so that there is nothing left to tie me down.

STEPH: Do those roots include people?

BARRY: I guess so.

STEPH (unenthused): That's really deep.

BARRY: But do you understand what I am saying?

STEPH: I'm not a dumbhead, Barry!

BARRY: Good. It's nice to talk to someone who can relate to what I'm saying. (They sit for some time in silence.) The wind's really starting to blow.

STEPH: Barry? (She glances at him, then stares off into the distance.) Barry—

BARRY: What?

STEPH: Do you ever . . . *(She stops.)* Do—

BARRY: What!?

STEPH: What do you think about me?

BARRY: What do you mean?

STEPH: I mean, what do you think about me?

BARRY: I think you're great.

STEPH *(upset):* You are such a creep sometimes. Please show some kind of emotions!

BARRY: *(He looks at her, then yells insanely.)* I think you're GREEEEAAAAT! *(He moans emotionally.)*

STEPH: Sometimes I really hate you.

BARRY: Well, what do you want me to say?

STEPH: Look—

BARRY: Yes.

STEPH: I have to tell you something.

BARRY: All right.

STEPH: I'm going away for the rest of the summer.

BARRY: What do you mean?

STEPH: I'm going to Europe with my grandparents.

BARRY: How long?

STEPH: Two months, maybe three.

BARRY: Well . . . when were you going to tell me this?

STEPH: I don't think I was.

BARRY: What do you mean?

STEPH: I'm leaving tomorrow.

BARRY: Well, why didn't you tell me?

STEPH: I guess I wanted to hurt you.

BARRY: Why did you want to hurt me?

STEPH: Because you have burned me off and on for the past four years.

BARRY: What do you mean?

STEPH: You have hurt me . . . really hurt me. I wanted to get you back.

BARRY: How have I hurt you?

STEPH: By not caring enough. By always being sort of there. I hate that detached air you have, like nothing can hurt you.

BARRY: Hey . . . I would go crazy if I didn't keep some sort of detached air. There is just too much to think about!

STEPH: Including me?

BARRY: Well, no . . . No! I think about you a lot.

STEPH: When?

BARRY: When I want—

STEPH (interrupting): When you want someone to listen to your stupid plays, or—

BARRY: Stop it! I'm not some jerk who uses you for—

STEPH: *(Jumps up.)* I don't want to talk about this.

BARRY: You're the one who brought it up!

STEPH: I am leaving. I have decided something. You will never understand how I feel about you.

BARRY: I thought we were friends.

STEPH: Friends . . . FRIENDS! Barry, I am in love with you.

BARRY: What?

STEPH: Yes . . . and I have been for quite some time. And every time you forgot to call or went out with some stupid girl, it hurt . . . really hurt. And do you know what? I don't even want to love you anymore. I don't even think I like you!

BARRY: Don't say that. How can you say that? I never thought you—

STEPH: That's the problem, you idiot! You can never tell people how you really feel about them. I have tried so many times to get some sort of—*(pause)* some reaction. But I'm through. I'm leaving. *(She starts to leave, then stops.)* Someday you are going to care about someone as much as I do about you, and then you will understand how I feel.

BARRY: Wait!

STEPH: Good-bye. *(She exits.)*

BARRY: *(He stands for some time. He looks around, frowning and moving his mouth silently.)* What happened? *(Pause.)* Creep? *(Beat.)* EUROPE!

(Blackout. Music-strings.)

SCENE THREE

A café in France. A café table sits downstage right with two chairs.
STEPHANIE *is at the table reading a book. She is wearing a summer dress. Behind the scrim is a cutout of a French cathedral. Lights up. A* WAITER *comes onstage and walks up to the table. He is the same waiter from the Zim Zam Café scene, although now his dress and demeanor are completely European.*

WAITER *(speaking incredibly fast):* Bonjour, mademoiselle. . . . Quesquevousavezcematin?

STEPH *(smiling):* Je besoin de café de crême.

WAITER: *(Snickers.)* Oh . . . you are A-merican. How lang have you been in Fronce?

STEPH: J'arrive un mois à Lyons.

WAITER *(grinning):* Please . . . spick English.

STEPH: Oh . . . great. Right. Uhhh. I've been here one month.

WAITER: Excellente! *(He stands for some time.)* Now, what would you like?

STEPH: *(She stares at him.)* Café de crême.

WAITER: *(Cocks his head.)* What do you say?

STEPH: Café de crême.

WAITER: *(Stares at her, then gives a little laugh.)* Ahhhhh. *(He gestures for her to follow his speech.)* Café de crrrrême. *(He says the word, thick with accent, making strange gurgling sounds in his throat.)* Écoutez. Café de crrrême.

STEPH: Café de crrrrême.

WAITER: Wonderful. *(He bows slightly.)* Enjoy your stay in our beautiful country. *(Exits.)*

(STEPH *goes back to reading. From stage left a* YOUNG MAN *enters. He is the same person who played* AGENT 4-H *in the Zim Zam scene. Now he is dressed like a college student, sunglasses around his neck, Stanford sweatshirt, chinos. He walks up to the table hesitantly.* STEPH *does not look up.)*

CRAIG: Uhhh . . . excuse moy, mad-moysly. I uhhh . . . je avez—

STEPH *(looking up):* What? I'm American.

CRAIG *(sighing):* Oh . . . *great!* *(Big pause.)* Me too. It's nice to meet someone from the States.

STEPH: Yeah. My name is Stephanie Eckert.

CRAIG: *(Sits down.)* Mine's Craig . . . Craig Strongman.

STEPH: How long have you been in Lyons?

CRAIG: About two weeks.

STEPH: How do you like it?

CRAIG: It's great. Except every time I try to speak French, they say, "What? What are you saying? Speak English." It's their way of getting us back.

STEPH: I know what you mean.

CRAIG: How long have you been here?

STEPH: About two months. In Europe, that is. I'm here with my grandparents. What are you doing here?

CRAIG: *(Slinks down in his seat, puts on the sunglasses, and looks around nervously.)* Actually *(pause)* I'm a spy.

STEPH *(startled):* What!?

CRAIG: *(Takes off glasses, laughs.)* I'm just kidding. Actually I'm heading down to Cannes *(says "cans")* for the film festival.

STEPH: Oh . . . *(Recovers herself from his joke.)* That's great. I always wanted to write screenplays and stuff. A friend *(beat)*, an ex-friend, that is, got me started on writing.

CRAIG: That's really cool. I want to be an actor, though. I guess I'm kind of a show-off.

STEPH *(coldly):* My friend was like that.

CRAIG: Gee, you must not have liked this . . . friend.

STEPH: No. I don't. In fact, I hate his guts!

CRAIG: What did he do to you?

STEPH: He broke my heart. *(Silence, then the two start laughing.)*

WAITER *(coming on with her coffee):* Enjoy your café. *(He gives CRAIG a patronizing stare, then walks off in a huff.)*

STEPH: So, where are you from, anyways?

CRAIG: I'm from Salinas, California. Where are you from?

STEPH: I'm from Ashland, Oregon.

CRAIG *(slapping his forehead with the palm of his hand):* Oh, wow! I've been there!

STEPH: Really?

CRAIG: Yeah. We go to the Shakespeare Festival there every year. *(Pause.)* How bizarre!

STEPH: That is weird. Pretty chance meeting, eh?

CRAIG: Yes. You know what? I even know someone in Ashland.

STEPH: Really?

CRAIG: Yeah. It's a guy. You see, last summer, I was driving up to Portland and my car wiped out.

STEPH: Oh, no—

CRAIG: Yeah. It was pretty bad. I broke my arm and had a skull fracture. But I probably would have died if it hadn't been for this guy who came out of nowhere, pulled me from the burning wreck, and drove me to the hospital!

STEPH: My gosh. What an incredible story. What was this guy's name, anyway?

CRAIG: It was Barry. *(Beat, then turns and gives his line directly to the audience:)* Barry Daniels.

STEPH: *(Stands up and throws her chair back, then fumes.)* What? That heartless creep! I hate him. He is my worst enemy!

CRAIG *(standing and facing her)*: Hey, hey—I can't have you talking that way about the guy who saved my life.

STEPH *(going crazy):* Shut up, you idiot! He is the biggest slob, jerk, dirtsucking, brainless—

CRAIG: Okay. That's it. *(He pulls out a revolver from his pants pocket.)* I'm going to have to shoot you. *(Points the gun at her.)*

STEPH *(looking up to the heavens, screaming):* Baaaaaaarrrrrrry! I hate yoooooooouuuu!

(The shot goes off. Blackout. A special comes up on BARRY as he jumps out of the wings onto the stage.)

BARRY *(writing furiously on a notepad):* Bye-bye, Stephy babe. Was nice knowing ya! *(Suddenly* STEPH *comes out of the darkness, grabs* BARRY's *arm, twists it behind his back, kicks his legs out from under him, presses his face into the floor.* BARRY *cries out in amazement.)* What in the—

STEPH: Your writing days are over, Buddy. *(Pushes harder on his back.)* Say uncle!

BARRY *(struggling)*: Never—

STEPH: *(Gives him a knee in the side.)* UNCLE!

BARRY *(screaming)*: No . . . No! I am writing this!! I am wri—

MOM *(offstage)*: BARRY! What in God's name are you doing!

BARRY: *(Looks up.)* Nothing, Mom. (STEPH *lets him go and exits silently.* BARRY *continues to struggle with his unseen nemesis.)*

MOM *(offstage)*: Where are you?

BARRY: *(Realizes the shadow figure is gone, jumps up.)* I'M IN MY ROOM!

(Lights come up. The set has been changed back to BARRY's *room.)*

MOM *(offstage)*: Barry. Don't you *ever* use that tone with me!

BARRY *(downcast)*: All right. Geez. I'm sorry.

MOM: What?

BARRY: All right. Okay. I'm sorry. *(Under his breath.)* Bite my head off.

(BEN *pokes his head into the room.)*

BEN: BEGAW! (BARRY *looks up at* BEN, *then sits at his desk and starts to type.* BEN *struts into the room.)* Hey, dude.

BARRY *(not looking up)*: Howzitgoin?

BEN: Oh, I'm all right.

BARRY: Good. Good. *(Stops typing and stares at* BEN.*)* Well, Ben, I can tell you have something to say.

BEN: Huh?

BARRY: Well, what is it? Is it about Stephanie?

BEN: Uhhhh. Yeah. As a matter of fact, it is. *(Plops down on the futon couch.)* I got a letter from her the other day.

BARRY: *(Types again.)* Oh? How is the world traveler?

BEN: She's having a great time. In fact, she thinks she wants to live there someday.

BARRY: Whooaaa. Wouldn't we all.

BEN: She's still pissed off at you.

BARRY *(startled):* What in the he— *(beat).* She's mad at me?

BEN: She told me all about the conversation before she left.

BARRY: Oh yeah?

BEN: Yeah. Gosh, Barry, you're one heckuva suave guy.

BARRY: Speak English.

BEN: Hey, I'm only telling you what she said.

BARRY: Well. What did she say?

BEN: No. Barry, I am not going to get in the middle of this.

BARRY: *(Crosses to futon couch.)* Just tell me! You little honis!

BEN: No.

BARRY: All right. *(Furious.)* Then get off my friggin' futon thing! *(He kicks it.)*

BEN *(laughing)*: You know what? You really are a jerk sometimes.

BARRY: Yes. I do know that. Because about every person in the world today has told me that about eight million times! *(Points to the dog photo on the bookshelf.)* My dog even hates me. *(Goes back to the desk, sits, and continues typing.)*

BEN: It's all those negative vibes you're putting out. Ya know? You just seethe anger.

BARRY *(shaking his head)*: I seethe, I seethe. *(Begins to seethe.)* I am the seething man.

(BEN walks around behind the desk, takes a pair of glasses off the shelf, and puts them on. Lights come on inside the lenses. BEN stands behind BARRY, leans over his shoulder.)

BEN: What are you writing?

BARRY: None of your stupid business.

BEN: Is it another play?

BARRY: Yes. Another moronic play. *(He rips the page from the typewriter, crosses to the futon couch, and sits.)*

BEN *(taking off the glasses)*: Whooooaaa. Where did you get all this anger?

BARRY: It's her.

BEN: Hey. I told you she was in love with you.

BARRY: No, you didn't.

BEN: Yes, I did, you bonehead. . . . I told you, and you said, "Naw, we're just good friends, that's all." Well, you blew it, pal, and now she hates your guts.

BARRY: Don't you think I feel bad?

BEN: Wait. The human wall has some emotions. This is unreal.

BARRY: I feel like a dirtball.

BEN: *(Crosses to the futon, kneels down.)* Do you love her?

BARRY: I . . . don't know.

BEN: Listen, Barry. I . . . the reason I came over here was because I just wanted to say . . . I'm here. If you wanted someone to talk to. I'm here. *(Stares at BARRY, puts his hand on BARRY's arm.)*

BARRY: *(Glares at him.)* What do you want me to do? *(Jerks his arm away.)* Butt-rub with you?

BEN: *(Nods his head, raises his hand as if to speak, stops himself.)* Here's her address. *(Tosses a piece of paper on the floor, exits.)*

BARRY: *(Sits for some time in silence. Starts to laugh.)* This is sooo boring. I hate plays. I really do. Plays are boring for the most part. Especially old Shakespeare. He could really drown you in dialogue. The only thing that kept Shakespeare from playwright oblivion was the fact that about fifty people got killed in every play. Some of the sword fights, though, are . . . *(He stops, smiles.)* Hey . . . that's an idea! A sword fight . . . a bloody sword fight!

(Adventure music erupts, the lights begin to dim.)

BARRY: Hey! *(Looking up.)* Don't I set the stage?

(The music stops, the lights come back up. BARRY grabs his notebook and walks to center stage.)

BARRY: Okay. The scene is in . . . *(pause)* France! Yeah . . . that's it.

(French music begins to play. As BARRY gives his speech, the lights dim to blackness except for the special above his head.)

BARRY: The evil duke of Normandy . . . Guy de Richmont . . . has seduced the beautiful girlfriend of the brave Englishman . . . Barry . . . Sebastien Barry of Gloucester and . . . the Lower Dubervilles. Richmont has brought her to Normandy, promising her his kingdom and all the Brie she could imagine. But the girl *(pause)*, Stephanie of Aragon, catches on to his plot and gets word to Barry with a cryptic message written on a slab of blue cheese. Barry takes off for France with his trustworthy, but extremely obnoxious manservant, Ben, and heads for Normandy in a rage of passion and fury, vowing to get Richmont really good.

(End music. BARRY exits. Lights up. As BARRY has been speaking, the stage has been cleared. BEN enters. He is dressed in Elizabethan regalia. He is carrying a backpack, several pots, a large sleeping roll, and a typewriter in carrying case. He stumbles to center stage, exhausted, stops, and sinks to his knees on the floor.)

BEN: My master, Sebastien Barry,
Comes sauntering hither thither—
From whence my pains of burden grow.
I feel weak with luggage carried 'cross the channel,
Everything from pots and swords to shirts of flannel.

My Master comes in a rage,
Ere this place of Frenchmen, a fight we'll wage.
To my heart dear Stephanie holds the key—
If it weren't for her, I'd surely flee.

BARRY *(offstage):* Ben? Where scurry thee?

BEN: Oh . . . 'tis my suffering to be a rube—
For my master is such a boob.
He constantly threatens and jibes and commands,
Methinks he has some problem with his glands.

(BARRY enters the stage riding a long stick as if it were a horse. He makes whinnying noises, gallops to center stage, stops, and pretends to sit atop his steed.)

BARRY: How now, Ben?
Why dost thou lie so low,

Likest a dog bestricken with the plague?
All panting and scraggly,
Bedraggled and loathsome.

BEN: Master, 'tis only for my burdens that I feel this way.

BARRY: Oh, do be gay,
'Tis a bright and cheery day.
I could make it worse you know.
Hit you, bruise you, give you a blow.

BEN: Oh, master, hit me not—
For my tender skin could scarce take a striking
From one as mighty as thou.

BARRY: Your praises do thou service to me,
But forget about that, there's Castle Normandy.

(BARRY *starts to trot away.*)

BEN: My master is a cruel and heartless fellow.

BARRY: What was that, dear Ben?

BEN *(getting up to leave):* Nothing, master. I follow.

(Exeunt BARRY *and* BEN *stage right. Enter* GUY *and* STEPHANIE. *They are dressed appropriately.* GUY *is running a knife over a whetstone.)*

STEPH: Guy?

GUY: Oui.
Stephanie?

STEPH: Dost thou lovest me likest thou hast sayed?
I must know, for my heart grows discontented.

GUY: But how, my tiny snail,
Could you doubt my heart's bewail?

I have given you the moon and sea—
Not to mention all that Brie.

STEPH: Guy, you are wicked and cruel,
And I thinkest you think of me a fool.

GUY: *(Stops whetting the knife, puts his hands on his hips.)*
Why sayest thou?

STEPH: I sayest I thinkest your intentions
Are not the greatest.

GUY: You hurt me with foolery.
You know how I feel,
With this kiss I doth seal— *(He kisses her.)*
For I have dear business to attend.
Ahh! Here is my servant, good man, and friend.

(BART, *dressed as a servant, peeks his head around the corner and gives* GUY *the "psssst" sign.)*

GUY: How now, good Bartholomew,
What hast thou to do?

BART *(smiling evilly):*
Good master, I needest speak wif you.

GUY *(to* STEPH*):* Kind temptress, you must leave us to chat
(Glances up and down her body.)
Please go and . . .
Play with your cat.

(STEPH *leaves, but stops by the door and listens to them speak.)*

GUY: Be quick, good Bart.

BART: Calm for the moment, master,
Listen to what's in store.
After you hear what I sayeth,
In haste you'll be more.

GUY: Do tell.

BART: Master, your enemy Barry comes sneaking.

(Pause, then GUY *and* BART *laugh together, maniacally.)*

GUY *(bellowing):*
Ohhhh! Glorious day at last.
I will crush him and kill him—
Bring him to his knees.
And when I am done—

BART *(beat):* Turn him to cheese.

(There is another long pause as GUY *takes in a deep breath, then explodes with laughter.* BART *holds out his hand—*GUY *takes his knife, puts the point on* BART's *palm, and gives the blade a sadistic twist.* BART *cries gleefully.* STEPH *lets out a little gasp.* BART *and* GUY *exit right, followed by* STEPH. BEN *and* BARRY *enter left.)*

BARRY: Hither ho, meek Ben.
You slow us down, 'twill take all day.

BEN *(staggering behind):*
Forgive me of my weaker traits,
But when death approaches, sometimes—
'Tis better to be late.

BARRY: What! You think I shall fail?

BEN: Well. To me a two-man siege does not sound like fun.
If it were up to me, we'd have brought a big gun.

BARRY: Silly Ben, so naive and meek.
Do you want me to slap at your cheek?
Assaulting and scaling is not our way.
We'll sneak in like shadows and steal my love away.

BEN: What if she doesn't like you anymore?

BARRY: Don't be daft and silly, man.

BEN: 'Tis only a thought.

BARRY: And one best left as one.

BEN: Master, a question—
As long as I'm thinking.

BARRY: Pray thee, get it over with.

BEN: Since stealth is the matter and essence of surprise,
Wouldn't it be better if I stayed outside?

BARRY: Dear God, have I heard you correct?
I am deeply hurt, my friend.
We are pals, you and I, to the end.

(BARRY *takes* BEN's *hand in his. They do a silly handshake.*)

I will hear no more, not a word.
Besides *(hands him the sword),*
Who will carry my sword?

(They depart. Lights dim. We are now in a church. Gregorian chant music comes up. A special shines in the shape of a cross on the floor. BART and GUY, dressed in robes, their faces covered with hoods, walk slowly from either side and meet in the middle. BART giggles and whispers, "Master." GUY slaps him in the head and gives the "shhh" sound. They walk upstage and stand silently. STEPHANIE enters. She walks up to the light, kneels, and begins to pray. From stage left BARRY enters, dressed in a priest's robe. His face is covered. Behind him BEN stands at the entrance, nervously glancing about. BARRY walks up behind STEPH and puts his hand on her shoulder.)

STEPH *(without turning around):* Oh, Father. I have confessions to make.

BARRY *(imitating the voice of an old priest):*
Yes, child. Do tell.

STEPH: I have wronged my true love in Britain.
Now my heart is broken and smitten.

BARRY *(overcome):* Oh, no, my dear child,
All is not lost,
For one's heart is wild—
With pain at no cost.
For one stands behind you, his throat all in lumps.
(His voice cracks and changes to his own.)
Turn around, Stephanie. I'm the one that you dumped.
(He throws back his hood.)

STEPH: *(Turns and looks at him.)* Oh, dear God. How many
times have I prayed.
Your face is like an angel. Am I in dreams?

BARRY: No, my sweet, I have traveled the miles—
And all for your kindly kisses and smiles.

(They embrace.)

BEN *(to the audience):* I'm the one doth deserve such reward.
Whilst he's off at parties,
I'm home alone, bored.

GUY *(taking a step forward):* Now's my chance to slice up this
looser.
Turn around, Barry. *(Throws back his hood.)*
Fight, you meek pooser.

(GUY throws off his robe and tosses it to BART. BARRY turns around and gasps as GUY takes out his sword.)

BEN: *(Tosses BARRY his sword.)* Barry! Watch out!

(BARRY and GUY fight a heated battle. They are both excellent swordsmen. At one point BART grabs STEPHANIE from behind and holds a knife to her throat. Then GUY envelopes BARRY's sword, spinning it around in a circle. GUY flings BARRY's sword away. BARRY, out of control, lunges the blade into BEN's chest.)

BEN (*crying out*): Begaw!

BARRY (*pulling the sword from Ben's body*): Ben! My friend. (BEN *falls to the floor, dead.* GUY *walks over and gives* BART *a "high five."* BARRY *becomes furious.*) Bloody French fiend!

GUY (*sneering*): Stupid (*pause*) writer!

(*They continue to fight. Near the end* GUY *backs* BARRY *into the wall, where* BART *is waiting with his knife.* STEPHANIE *screams* BARRY'*s name.* BARRY *dodges the knife and slices* BART *across the stomach.*)

BART (*falling to the ground*): Master!

(GUY *walks over to* STEPH, *grabs her by the hair, and drags her to the other side of the stage.* BARRY *is frozen with horror.* GUY *pulls back* STEPH'*s head and kisses her unmercifully.*)

BARRY (*screaming*): DARRNNIT! (BARRY *lunges forward, off balance, and* GUY *grabs his sword by the blade and plucks it away. Then* GUY *brings his sword down as if to cleave* BARRY *in two.* BARRY *escapes the blow, grabs his sword from* GUY'*s hand, and strips it cruelly from* GUY'*s fingers.* BARRY *brings his sword across* GUY'*s Achilles tendon, and the evil* DUKE *falls to his knees. He grabs* GUY'*s head and places the blade to his neck. He turns to* STEPH.) Run! (BARRY *jerks back* GUY'*s head.*) Now, Richmont . . . the victory is mine. (*He pulls the blade across* GUY'*s throat.* GUY *crashes to the floor.* BARRY *runs to center stage, takes* STEPH'*s hand and turns to go.*) Come, Stephanie. Let's away. (*Suddenly* GUY *lets out a low moan, "Aaaauuuuggghhhh!" He sits up, looks at the audience, takes out a knife, points the hilt at* STEPHANIE'*s chest, and flings back his arm.* BARRY *watches helplessly as the knife travels across the stage.* STEPHANIE *clutches her breast, a knife stuck in her chest. She lets out a little gasp, pulls out the knife, lets it drop to the floor, then faints backward.* BARRY *catches her in his arms. He lets her fall gently to the floor. Carefully, he folds her little hands across her stomach and leans over her dead body. Forlornly:*) Oh, God! Why couldn't I . . . Why couldn't I tell you . . . touch your face . . . kiss your lips . . . your hair. (*Touches her hand.)* Your hands are so small. The first time I saw you— *(Stops, looks up with anguish, doing his best King Lear.)*

Oh, that a parrot, a squirrel, a giraffe should have life—
And not my Stephanie.
I would give—

MOM *(offstage):* Barry! Come outside and help me move these planters. Hurry up!

BARRY *(breaking character):* Okay. In a minute. *(Looks back up.)* That a man such as I could ever feel—

MOM *(offstage):* Barry, where are you?

BARRY: *(Moans.)* All right! Ahhhh . . . bloody . . . crap! I can never finish anything. *(Gets up to leave.)* I am slave to the world. *(Exit BARRY.)*

BEN: *(After several seconds, BEN stirs, then gets up. He looks around for a moment, then nudges STEPH.)* Pssst! Hey . . . he's gone.

STEPH: *(Jumps up.)* Oh, good. Now we can have some fun.

(Elizabethan music erupts. GUY and BART jump up. The FOUR do a zany parody of an Elizabethan dance. All of them laugh and smile as they sing.)

BEN: Barry's gone, Barry's gone—
Now we'll have some fun, fun, fun!

ALL: He's a bore, such a bore
Start the party, Barry's gone.

BEN: Barry is a hopeless geek.

ALL: Nonny, nonny, nonny, no.

BEN: Ugly, daft, and weak.

ALL: Nonny, nonny, nonny, no.

STEPH: Heartless—

GUY: Insensitive—

BART: Stupid—

BEN: And lame—

ALL: If he were someone else,
He would say the same!

(They dance together as the lights go out.)

SCENE FOUR

A month later at the park. A park bench has been brought out. Lights come up. BEN is sitting on the bench. STEPH comes onto the stage. He pretends not to see her. She kicks his foot. He laughs, grabs her, and they hug.

BEN: God. It's good to see you.

STEPH: I know. It's good to be home.

BEN: *(Lets go of her. Stands back a little and looks at her.)* Did you get my message?

STEPH: Yes, but I couldn't get away from everyone. How long have you been waiting?

BEN: A couple of minutes. *(Pause.)* Okay. An hour . . . maybe two.

STEPH: I'm sorry.

BEN: It's all right. September is nice. I like being outside.

STEPH: *(They both sit down.)* I really missed you. *(Takes a deep breath.)* It's so nice to be sitting in one spot. Grandpa and Grandma are on speed or something. They wore me out.

BEN: Well—

STEPH: Well—

BEN: Tell me about it.

STEPH: *(She starts to take off her shoes, peels down her socks.)* It was incredible. I've never felt so free. We would just go someplace, and if we didn't like it, we'd hop on a train and leave. *(She pulls a brown paper cutout in the shape of her foot out of her sock.)*

BEN: What's that? *(Takes the cutout from her hand, holds it up.)*

STEPH: That was Grandpa's idea. He saw it on *Merv Griffin.* He said that if you cut out grocery bags in the shape of your feet and wear them under your socks, you won't get jet lag.

BEN: Did it work?

STEPH: *(Lets out a little laugh.)* I did it for Grandpa. He did pay for the trip.

BEN: So, what was the most interesting thing that happened to you?

STEPH: Oh . . . I think it was how, wherever I went, I kind of wanted to melt into that culture . . . sort of disappear. You know, start dressing and acting like those people.

BEN: Like pretend you weren't with your grandpa and grandma.

STEPH: No. They were fun. Fun and fast. They wanted their money's worth out of everything. *(Pause.)* So, what did you do this summer?

BEN: I've been working a lot. It has been incredibly boring. I'm not trying to make you feel guilty or anything.

STEPH: It's all right. I'm through feeling guilty about anything.

BEN: Good.

STEPH: So, how's what's his name?

BEN: I haven't talked to him in about a month. *(Silence.)*

STEPH: Did you give him that one address?

BEN: Yes. *(Pause.)* Did you ever write him?

STEPH: No.

BEN: Stephanie?

STEPH: What?

BEN: You two are so stupid.

STEPH: How so?

BEN: I mean . . . both of you. You're going to regret not keeping in touch with each other. Just listen to me for a minute. You . . . you two are so stubborn. You know, it wasn't his fault alone that you . . . whatever. I mean—

STEPH: Listen, Ben. I know what you are trying to do. It's all right. Both of us will live.

BEN: I know . . . but . . . when you have friends, you shouldn't just drop them.

STEPH: Ben, I'm only eighteen. I'm young. I don't feel anything for him anymore.

BEN: I'm not talking about love. I'm talking about— *(Stops.)* When certain people get together and they talk, just being around each other . . . it's like . . . sparks. You can see that energy . . . you know . . . they just sort of—

STEPH: And Barry and I spark when we're together?

BEN: Yes. Sort of. You kind of fuel each other. But what I'm saying is that you should just remember, because twenty years from now . . .

(He stops as BARRY comes onstage. STEPH doesn't look at BARRY.)

BEN: I've got to go. *(He kisses her on the cheek.)* It was great talking to you.

BARRY *(before BEN exits):* Ben? I'm sorry—

BEN: It's okay. *(He leaves.)*

BARRY: *(Walks up to the bench.)* Hi. I wanted to talk to you before you left for school.

STEPH: That's good.

BARRY: I missed . . . *(pause)* I miss—

STEPH: *(Cuts him off.)* So. How was your summer?

BARRY: It was all right.

STEPH: Good.

BARRY: How was the trip?

STEPH: Good.

BARRY: So. When do you go to school?

STEPH: Next weekend. How about you?

BARRY: Week after.

STEPH: Oh. *(Pauses.)* Did you finish your play?

BARRY: Sent it off today.

STEPH: Great. That's really great. Do you think you'll win?

BARRY: No. But I'm glad I tried. At least I won't regret it someday.

STEPH: Barry, I'm sorry for slamming you before I left.

BARRY: No. It was my fault. I deserved it. *(Pause.)* Steph. I don't want to regret anything . . . ever—

STEPH: Me neither.

BARRY: I have to say something.

STEPH: No. Barry . . . please, I have to go.

BARRY: I have to, Steph. After you left, I realized what a jerk I was. I have been afraid my entire life of ever telling anyone how I felt about them. No. Not just telling someone, but giving them a part of myself. I know it sounds cheesy, but—

STEPH: Barry . . . don't.

BARRY: Just listen. *(She gets up.)* I love you. Maybe not in the way you would have wanted me to . . . but I don't know. *(She starts to go.)* Wait! I have to know how you feel.

STEPH: I'm sorry. I don't think I feel for you the way I did before. Because . . . you have to understand . . . it hurts too much. I think I would rather hate you than fall in love with you again.

BARRY: Why?

STEPH: *(Looks at him.)* Because it's too much.

BARRY: I've figured out a lot of things this summer. The people you know . . . they are the most important thing in your life. You can either hide from them or be willing to— *(Stops.)* I'm not afraid of being hurt!

(She runs offstage. He watches her, then walks over to the bench and sits. Sad music comes up softly. BARRY *looks at the audience.)*

BARRY: In school they told me a play was a plot, characters, and action. But I have discovered that it is far more. I think that if someone goes through the trouble to write a play, even if everyone hates it, if one person is touched by something said, it's worth the trouble. Because the most important things a writer can write about are those which happen to him . . . really happen. *(Holds up his arms.)* I wrote a play! *(Looks down.)* But what happened to the happy ending?

(As the music rises to its ending, STEPH *walks onto the stage. She goes up to the bench and sits down next to* BARRY. *He stares at her as if seeing a dream . . . an image . . . a character in his imagination. Behind them, a curtain rises, unveiling the scrim. We see a field . . . a house on a hill . . . trees . . . and the sun going down. Blackout.)*

NOBLE MASON SMITH

When I was a very young boy, a psychic prophesied to my parents that in my life I would be speaking to a great number of people. My dad assumed this meant I was to be a door-to-door vacuum salesman. Fortunately this has not come to pass. The Indian mystics warn, "Whatever you desire will come to you." Well, I wished to be a writer. It was a yearning realized with the winning of the Young Playwrights Festival. The experience, however fantastic, was painful. I hated New York. If I could do it again, I would probably still hate New York, but certainly then I was too young to enjoy being on my own in such a monumental place. It was, though, one of the most thrilling events of my life to actually see real, live people live my words. Everyone at Playwrights Horizons was thoroughly professional, maybe a little too professional. The script went through numerous changes—albeit good ones. But the pressure I sometimes felt to succeed was so great, it made me wish I had never written the ridiculous thing after all. For me, working with professional actors and a talented director was fantastic. Several of the funniest lines in the play were made up by the actors. This is something most writers will never admit. They will say, and I agree, that the play is a vehicle, and without the initial work, none of the additional things would ever have been invented. But I must say, actors are imaginative people, and I was enthusiastic to let them develop their characters, to grow and make them into something personal and creative.

The day after opening night I was bombarded with opportunities. On the same afternoon, I met and signed with an agent, pitched story ideas to a cheesy TV executive, and met with an editor at Samuel French to have my play published. On the way back to my apartment I was grinning like a fool. And why shouldn't I be happy? I thought. I had seen my name in *The New York Times*—a good review at that! I was going to be a published author. I was going to have an agent . . . MORE PLAYS! SCREENPLAYS! MONEY! NO MORE COLLEGE! I'LL TRAVEL THE WORLD! Suddenly, an odd-looking man stepped out of the awning of a building. He had scraggly hair, a bloated face, and distant eyes. He staggered in front of me. I stopped for a moment. He looked at me and grinned, held out his hand. "I'm just a playwright down on his luck," he muttered. I felt a rush of adrenaline in my chest. I walked away quickly. How about that? I thought. That was so profound, I couldn't even have written anything profounder! I shuddered at this strange meeting and took it as a voice of wisdom from on high.

I have written several screenplays, two plays, and lots of garbage since my New York days. I am a senior at the University of Michigan. I'm still waiting to score again.

CHILDREN

by Debra Terri Neff
(age sixteen when play was written)
Jamaica Estates, New York

NOTE:
For the purpose of publication in this collection, certain words
have been changed by the playwright, and some profanity has been
deleted from the working script of the play as performed at Playwrights Horizons, New York City, October 4 through 8, 1987.

Children was performed as part of the Chapman readings series at Playwrights Horizons, October 4–8, 1987, directed by Charles Karchmer. Wendy Wasserstein was the playwright adviser. The cast:

JENNY	Jill Tasker
MILLIE	Noelle Parker
JULIA	Leslie Lyles
SUZANNE	Elaine Bromka
DYLAN	Steve Larson

Children was written for Nancy Fales-Garrett's playwriting class at Saint Ann's School in Brooklyn in 1986. It was first performed at the Saint Ann's School Playwrighting Festival on June 5 and 6, 1986.

SCENE ONE

Jenny's bedroom, in a Manhattan apartment. The room is a mess with clothes and boxes everywhere. JENNY *stands on a chair shuffling through a box of papers in the closet,* MILLIE *sits in a corner of the bed surrounded by stuff, including an old, moldy terrarium.*

JENNY: Agh! Watch out! *(Box falls.)* Darn.

MILLIE: Are you okay?

JENNY: Uh-huh.

MILLIE: I don't understand why you're unpacking all this if your mother isn't forcing you.

JENNY: Look at this place, Millie. What's it been now, a month? I can't live like this. It's unhealthy. Like that terrarium, for example.

MILLIE: I think it's growing mold.

JENNY: It's a relic from our childhood. Remember when we had to make those?

MILLIE: Fourth grade. And yours was the biggest.

JENNY: Mine was the best and it got shown at the science fair. *(She climbs down and onto a pile of papers. She surveys the room.)* What a mess.

MILLIE: Maybe you should just take a big Hefty bag and shove everything in.

JENNY: Yeah, but what if I throw out something important.

MILLIE: So, you're going to sort through all this stuff?

JENNY *(kicking papers, etc., under the bed and out of the way)*:
Someday.

MILLIE: You're so lucky your mom never makes you do anything like clean your room.

JENNY: My mom never makes me do anything at all.

MILLIE: I just don't understand you. You were so psyched to live with your mom. Now that you're here, all you do is complain.

JENNY: Oh sure, because she was so much fun when I would visit her, but I never really knew her. The first few days I was here, I was so careful, leaving notes and telling her where I was going, and finally she said, "Listen, I don't need to know where you are twenty-four hours a day," and she gave me a big speech on respecting each other's privacy and freedom.

MILLIE: Cool.

JENNY: At least with Dad he knew I was alive. He was a pain in the butt, but he knew I was alive.

MILLIE: Do you really miss him?

JENNY: Yeah. But he said I could go to Kenya this summer and visit him.

MILLIE: Ooo, I bet it's hot there during the summer. I think I'll change my name.

JENNY: Why?

MILLIE: I hate my name. It sounds so icky . . . old. Like Mildew. Remember that boy in second grade that used to call me Mildew?

JENNY: What am I going to do with this terrarium? *(She exits with it.)*

MILLIE: Well, I'm way past the second-grade mildew. I need something now. Something eighties.

JENNY *(reentering without it):* I like your name.

MILLIE: How about . . . Dominique.

JENNY: No way. The girl in *Fame* changed her name to Dominique.

MILLIE: Oh. Dominella? Dominita? How about April?

JENNY: Or May, or June. How about December? I was born then.

MILLIE: No, that's tacky. I need something classy. Something with pizzazz.

JENNY: Oh, well then, why don't you just name yourself after a city in Italy?

MILLIE: Venice. Rome. Florence?

JENNY: I have an aunt named Florence, and I despise her. What about something from nature, like Heather?

MILLIE: Naaaa.

JENNY: Brooke.

MILLIE: Shields?

JENNY: Rose.

MILLIE: My grandmother's name is Rose.

JENNY: Chrysanthemum? Zinnia.

MILLIE: *Breeze!*

JENNY: What?

MILLIE: *Breeeeeeeze!* It's perfect! It's original, it's exciting, it . . . it . . .

JENNY: Has pizzazz?

MILLIE: Do you like it?

JENNY: It will take me a while to get used to it.

MILLIE: If it's really me, it should be easy.

JENNY: Oh, right.

(JULIA, *Jenny's mother, enters dressed very fancy. She twirls around.*)

JULIA: How do I look?

MILLIE: Beautiful.

JULIA: Oh, thank you, Millie.

JENNY: Where are you going?

JULIA: The health club.

JENNY: Why are you so dressed up?

JULIA: Well, there's this gorgeous exercise instructor and . . . I'm going to Dennis's house.

JENNY: When will you be back?

JULIA: Well, I don't know. Let's see . . . I got some of that crabmeat salad you said you like . . . and there's some ice cream, Tofutti actually, in the freezer. And I stopped at Zabar's and got some croissants, . . . but if you'd rather go out for breakfast, I can give you money . . .

JENNY: No, no, it's fine. Thanks.

JULIA: I mean, it isn't as though you're a child who can't manage without me, right? *(Pause.)* Well, I have to go. Give me kiss. *(She kisses both girls.)*

MILLIE: New perfume?

JULIA: Yes. It's Opium. Do you like it?

MILLIE: Yes. Can I borrow some?

JULIA: My babies are growing up. It's on my night table.

MILLIE: Thanks! *(She runs out.)*

JULIA: Sure. Well, ah, good-bye, Jen. Are you sure you'll be all right?

JENNY: Yes, of course.

JULIA: Well, 'bye. *(She exits. The apartment door slams.)*

JENNY: No, I won't be okay, Mom. What if the apartment gets robbed? What if your stupid Tofutti was poisoned? What if . . .

MILLIE *(reentering):* That's an eighties mom you got there, Jenn.

JENNY: Ugh, you smell just awful.

MILLIE: Oh yeah? Well, we'll see if it will get us served at Caramba tonight.

JENNY: We will never get served at Caramba, Millie, it's been seven months. They know us.

MILLIE: Put your hair back in that knot. Do you think your mom will mind if I borrow her sparkly sweater?

JENNY: I'm sure she won't.

MILLIE: Good. Do you have any tissues?

JENNY *(picks up box on desk):* Oh, no. I'm out. Are you wearing any now?

MILLIE: Yeah.

JENNY: Well, can't you just reuse them?

MILLIE: Oh, that's gross.

JENNY: Sorry, I'm no authority on bra stuffing. There's toilet paper in the bathroom.

MILLIE: *(Sighs.)* It'll do. *(She starts to exit, but stops by the mirror and strikes a dramatic pose.)* Breeze. *(She slumps.)* More and better tissues . . . maybe I'll get silicone implants.

JENNY: But Millie. . . . (MILLIE *is gone.*) We're only children.

SCENE TWO

Jenny's bedroom again. MILLIE *and* JENNY *enter.* MILLIE *looks positively devastated, and* JENNY *is carrying a pint of Tofutti.* MILLIE *collapses on* JENNY's *bed.* JENNY *takes off her shoes and starts brushing her hair.*

MILLIE: I'm so depressed.

JENNY: Oh, will you shut up already? All the way home, that's all I hear. I'm so depressed I'm so depressed I'm so depressed. . . . Have some Tofutti.

MILLIE: How can you eat Tofutti when our childhoods have been so abruptly ended?

JENNY: Why? Because we got served?

MILLIE: We're through. We're over the hill. Past our prime.

JENNY: How can you be past your prime when you're still stuffing your bra?

MILLIE: Don't you see? Our lives have no more purpose.

JENNY: Okay, so you're trying to tell me the entire purpose of our lives was to get served at Caramba?

MILLIE: Well, no . . . but now we don't have another adolescent challenge.

JENNY: Big deal. Let's get arrested for something.

MILLIE: Jenny, how can you be so . . . so . . . I mean, do you realize the psychological implications of this event?

JENNY: Yes. It made you very crazy.

MILLIE: Oh! *(She throws herself on the bed.)* I need to get away.

JENNY: You're wrinkling before my eyes.

MILLIE: Stop being so mean. I think you need to get away too. I think we both need some . . . some . . . fun in the sun.

JENNY: Oh no.

MILLIE: Look at me, Jen. I'm tense. I'm uptight. I need a vacation away from the pressures of adolescenthood and . . . parents.

JENNY: What?

MILLIE: Oh, Jenny, you're so lucky your mother never tries to cramp your style! My parents have me so brainwashed, I'm absolutely . . . I'm beat. I need to find myself.

JENNY: You need to what?

MILLIE: Find myself. Well, I guess you don't have that problem, but you can come along anyway, and your mom. We'll go to . . . California. Visit your mom's friend. Weave hammocks, join a commune, and generally leave behind our bourgeois counterparts and experience a clandestine subculture.

JENNY: A what?

MILLIE: We have to do it now, before we hit college and the real world. We have to be ready for our postadolescences. Are you listening to me?

JENNY: Do you think I should get my hair cut?

MILLIE: Does your mom's friend live on a commune?

JENNY: Try condo.

MILLIE: Do you think we can convince your mom to go see her?

JENNY: We could probably convince my mom to go to the North Pole as long as there would be men there.

(JULIA *enters, depressed, and collapses on a chair.*)

JULIA: I. Hate. Men.

JENNY: What happened?

JULIA: That louse. That rat. That . . . that . . . slime. Do you know what he said?

JENNY: No, what did he say?

JULIA: Give me that Tofutti. He said . . . he said . . . oh, forget it. I'm going to get drunk and then I'm going to bed. *(She starts to exit, but* MILLIE *brings her back and sits her down.)*

MILLIE: Julia, Julia. Look at yourself. You're tired, you're depressed. I think what you need is a vacation. Think of it, Julia, California. Visiting your friend out there. Seeing the sights with your lovely daughter and her best friend. The beaches. The surfers. The lifeguards.

JULIA: California?

MILLIE: Well, sure. Wouldn't it be nice to see . . . uh . . .

JENNY: Suzanne.

MILLIE: Suzanne. To tell Suzanne what he said.

JULIA: California's awfully expensive.

MILLIE: Oh, come on. Isn't it a mere pittance to spend for rest, rejuvenation, vacation?

JULIA: Mmmm.

MILLIE: And Jenny and me will go with you. For moral support.

JULIA: I guess Jenny told you Suzanne has a son named Pierre who's only a little older than you. (MILLIE *laughs.*) Well, do you think your parents would let you?

MILLIE: Well, my parents aren't as nice as you, Julia. Maybe you'd have to talk to them.

JULIA: Oh, I don't know about that. I'm always very nervous talking to parents, Millie.

JENNY: Millie changed her name to Breeze.

JULIA: Excuse me?

JENNY: Millie changed her name to Breeze.

JULIA: That's a very nice name, Millie.

MILLIE: Thank you. So, ah . . . what about California?

JULIA: Well, it sounds very tempting, but you know I can't just pick up and run off like that.

MILLIE: So, you're not going to go.

JULIA: No, no, I never said that. It's just that . . . well, I want to, but . . .

MILLIE: What's wrong with taking a vacation? You work hard. We all work hard. We need time to take in the sun, perhaps engage in a cross-cultural romance . . .

JULIA: Why don't you ask your parents about it, Millie? Maybe we can work something out. Do you want to go, Jenny?

JENNY: Yeah. I guess.

JULIA: Well, I'll look into it. I'm going to bed. (*She exits, then runs back and grabs the Tofutti.*)

JENNY: Good night, Mom. (*Pause.*) Good night, Mom!

JULIA (*offstage*): What? Oh, me. Good night.

SCENE THREE

A row of three seats on an airplane. MILLIE *is asleep, resting her head against the window.* JENNY *sits in the middle, and* JULIA *at the end, listening to her Walkman and smoking a Salem Menthol 100 cigarette.* JENNY *reaches for* JULIA's *lighter.*

JENNY: Can I have a cigarette, Mom? *(She doesn't hear.* JENNY *taps her. She takes her headphones off.)*

JULIA: Yes?

JENNY: Can I have a cigarette?

JULIA: Oh, sure.

JENNY: Thanks.

JULIA: Sure. *(She puts her headphones back on.* JENNY *opens the ashtray and flicks ash in. She glances at* MILLIE, *then back at* JULIA.)

JENNY: Mom? *(She doesn't hear.* JENNY *taps her.)* Julia?

JULIA: *(Takes her headphones off.)* Yes?

JENNY: Will you tell me what he said?

JULIA: What? Oh, Dennis?

JENNY: Yeah.

JULIA: Oh. Nothing.

JENNY: Why won't you tell me?

JULIA: Well, ah . . . no reason, I guess. I mean, it doesn't matter, right?

JENNY: Yeah.

JULIA: I mean, I'll tell you if you're really curious.

JENNY: Oh, no, I don't care.

JULIA: Well, anyway, it was ludicrous. And totally unjustified.

JENNY: Oh.

JULIA: I mean, we were having a perfect relationship. We'd go to dinner, or a show, or just to his house. Really nice. Easy, right? No complications. I thought he was happy that way, but he's . . . he's crazy, Jen. He said he feels our relationship lacks the relationship part. He feels there's no give-and-take and all that other women's-magazine crap. He said . . . he said he didn't think I was MATURE enough to have a serious relationship!

JENNY: Oh.

JULIA: He's crazy. He doesn't know a good thing when he has one.

JENNY: Oh.

(JULIA *puts her headphones back on.*)

JENNY: Well, couldn't you try it, Mom?

(Takes them off.)

JULIA: What?

JENNY: Couldn't you try it, Mom?

JULIA: Try what?

JENNY: Try to, like . . . have a serious relationship.

JULIA: Well, we were.

JENNY: Oh.

JULIA: Dennis is a putz.

JENNY: I liked him.

JULIA: Listen, Jen, I know in a few years you're going to want to start going out with boys, so I'll give you all my motherly advice now: Don't. Become a lesbian or something. *(She gets up.)* I'm going to the bathroom.

(MILLIE has waked up. She and JENNY look at each other, then make a passionate lunge for each other, laughing hysterically.)

SCENE FOUR

Suzanne's living room. SUZANNE *and* JULIA *are sitting on the couch drinking frothy health shakes and looking at a copy of* Mademoiselle.

SUZANNE: First they do a whole issue: "Skinny girls ain't sexy," and then they show us clothes you have to be a twig to wear.

JULIA: I know! I hate it! I wish everyone would make up their minds about who they want us to be.

SUZANNE: Well, right here they do. They have defined the eighties woman and they show three examples.

JULIA: It's so eerie how you always know what I mean. I'm so glad I came out here. I just needed to get away. I mean, life is so *confusing.* Look at this! Have a job, have a lover, have a baby, learn to cook, teach him to cook, learn to make love, teach him to make love, have another baby, get divorced, sleep with your ex, move to the suburbs, move back to the city.

SUZANNE: Don't pay any attention to it. I don't even read the stuff myself.

JULIA: I don't know why I do.

SUZANNE: I guess you feel you need some sort of guide to life.

JULIA: Well, who should I ask? You say relax and find yourself, Dennis says act your age, my mother says be a daughter she can tell her friends about, Jenny says . . . oh, God knows what Jenny says . . .

SUZANNE: Julia, Julia, just be yourself.

JULIA: But I can't just be myself when I'm not sure who I am and everyone around me has a different idea.

SUZANNE: Okay, but, Julia, now you're away from everyone else, we even put the girls in a hotel so you wouldn't have them to bother you, and I'm on your side. By the time you leave, you should have yourself straightened out.

JULIA: I feel like I should pay you by the hour.

SUZANNE: I don't love any of my patients like I love you.

JULIA: Oh, thank you. *(They hug.)*

SUZANNE: And now, I have something very important to show you, and I've been saving it all this time, and it's not going to wait another minute! *(She gets up and runs to the armoire. She comes out struggling with an oversized box of clothes, which she drops on the floor.)*

JULIA: Oooo! Clothes! Let's play dress-up! *(She jumps up and goes to kneel by the box. She holds up a pink taffeta prom dress.)* I remember this! Does it still fit?

SUZANNE: No way. Maybe it'll fit you. You go to a health club, don't you?

JULIA: Yeah. *(They hold up that dress.)* Oh, no way. Forget it. Look at that waist! It's eensy. Were we ever that small? *(Scream, holds up a slinky black dress.)* Oh, my God, I can't believe you kept this!

SUZANNE: Oh, how could I ever throw it out!

(JENNY wanders in.)

JULIA: Do you think it would fit Jenny?

JENNY: What?

SUZANNE: Ooo, Jenny.

JULIA: Ooo, Jenny.

(They circle like sharks.)

SUZANNE: Jenny's so pretty.

JENNY: Well, don't hold it against me. I'll grow out of it soon.

JULIA: I wish I had a tiny waist like that.

SUZANNE: It must be so much fun to be fifteen. I bet you have a lot of boyfriends.

JULIA: Oh, she does.

JENNY: No, I don't.

SUZANNE: Well, maybe if this dress . . . *(She holds the slinky dress up against JENNY.)* Oh, look! It will fit.

JULIA: Oh, I'm just dying to see it on! *(JULIA starts to undress JENNY.)* JENNY: Hey! I'll do it, okay? *(She grabs the dress and storms into the bedroom.)*

SUZANNE: Let's give her the prom dress next.

JULIA: Yeah.

SUZANNE: Oh, I wish Pierre were a girl so I could dress him up. I did when he was a baby, but now he just won't take it. You're so lucky you have a daughter, Julia.

JULIA: Yeah, I know. I just can't believe you still have that dress. I remember all those times we wore it.

SUZANNE: You borrowed it for your first date with that guy . . . what was his name? You went to some fancy bar and got served.

JULIA: Right! I came home drunk, and my mother almost killed me. Let's see . . . oooo . . . started with an *S.*

SUZANNE: Right.

JULIA: *Lester!*

SUZANNE: Right!

JULIA: *Lester Boggs!*

SUZANNE: We thought he was so wonderful!

JULIA: What a catch! He was so stupid!

SUZANNE: But cute. With those T-shirts.

JULIA: And the holes in the jeans. Who was that guy you were seeing?

SUZANNE: Troy.

JULIA: That couldn't have been his real name.

SUZANNE: No. (JENNY *reenters, in the slinky dress.*) Julia, she could be you! Ready to go a bar with Lester Boggs.

JULIA: Only she doesn't have to worry about her mother catching her and asking where she's going. I must have a picture of this. Let me get my camera. (*She runs off.*)

JENNY: I feel ridiculous.

SUZANNE: Don't be silly, darling. Here, let me brush your hair. (*She gets a brush.*) What beautiful hair!

JENNY: Thank you.

(JULIA *returns.*)

JULIA: Okay, now, stand together. (SUZANNE *puts her arm around* JENNY *and smiles.* JULIA *takes the picture.*)

SUZANNE: Okay, now one of you two. (JULIA *and* JENNY *stand awkwardly together while* SUZANNE *takes the picture.*)

JULIA: Okay, now which one? The prom dress?

SUZANNE *(handing it to* JENNY*)*: Ooo, yes! (JENNY *takes the dress and runs out of the room.*)

SUZANNE: Oh, she's going to look so beautiful!

JULIA: I can't wait for these pictures.

SUZANNE: You'll have to send me copies.

JULIA: Well, can't I get them developed here?

SUZANNE: Oh, of course. And we'll just order extra copies.

JULIA: Right. Is there any more of that health shake?

SUZANNE: Let's go make some more. *(They start toward the kitchen.)* I'll show you my secret ingredient. (JENNY *sneaks in, still wearing the dress. She looks around, then grabs a key from the ashtray on the table and runs out. The door slams, but it can barely be heard over a loud crash, a scream of* "carob soy milk," *a blender, and hysterical giggles.*)

SCENE FIVE

A playground outside a condominium. JENNY *runs on, looks around, finds what she's looking for offstage, and shouts.*

JENNY: MILLIE! *(Waves.* MILLIE *runs in.)*

MILLIE: Don't call me Millie. What is with the dress?

JENNY: I've been looking all over for you.

MILLIE: Yeah, I know. Dylan told me you called him there twice looking for me.

JENNY: Yeah.

MILLIE: Anything going on with you two?

JENNY: Maybe. Yeah. Sort of. I guess.

MILLIE: That's great! He's really nice.

JENNY: He's okay.

MILLIE: And he's really cute.

JENNY: He's okay!

MILLIE: Well, were you looking for me for any special reason?

JENNY: Yeah, you disappeared.

MILLIE: Yeah. Well, Pierre's friends are pretty cool. Especially Todd.

JENNY: Todd's nice.

MILLIE: Yeah! What time does your mom want us to be back at the hotel?

JENNY: She doesn't care, of course.

MILLIE: Okay, see you later.

JENNY: Mill . . . Breeze. Wait.

MILLIE: What?

JENNY: Stay with me.

MILLIE: Why?

JENNY: Because.

MILLIE: Why don't you come with us? We're all going to Dylan's house later.

JENNY: No, I don't want to see him.

MILLIE: Oh.

JENNY: Why don't we just go back to the hotel? There's a really good ice-cream store. We could . . . oh, I don't know. Get some food, stay up, and talk.

MILLIE: Naaa, I don't feel like it. Why don't you want to hang out?

JENNY: Oh, I don't know. I don't like most of Pierre's friends. They smell. And Dylan makes me nervous the way he's always hanging on me.

MILLIE: Oh, don't be such a child, Jenny. Dylan is perfectly nice and he smells fine and he doesn't hang on you any more than any normal guy hangs on his girlfriend.

JENNY: Well, I'm not his girlfriend, and it makes me nervous.

MILLIE: You're really crazy. You really are. Good-bye. Go home.

JENNY: I don't want to be alone.

MILLIE: Then go to Suzanne's house.

JENNY: I can't.

MILLIE: Why not?

JENNY: Because Suzanne and Julia are acting like children.

MILLIE: What did they do?

JENNY: They started dressing me up in their old clothes like I was some kind of Barbie doll. It was really scary.

MILLIE: Hence the dress. Well, they were just having fun. Sick fun, but . . .

JENNY: They were acting like *children!* Aren't there any *grown-ups* anywhere?

MILLIE: I don't know what you're talking about. Are you tripping?

JENNY: No, I'm not tripping!

MILLIE: Go back to the hotel, Jenny. Get a good night's sleep. You'll feel better in the morning.

JENNY: Will you stop acting like you're my mother!

MILLIE: I thought that's what you wanted! *(She storms off.)*

SCENE SIX

Dylan's very cluttered apartment. DYLAN *asleep on the couch. Door-bell.* DYLAN *groans but gets up and stumbles over to answer the door. It is* JENNY.

DYLAN: Oh! Jenny. Hi.

JENNY: Hi.

(Then together:)

DYLAN: I didn't know you . . .

JENNY: Sorry I didn't . . .

(Pause.)

DYLAN: I didn't know you knew where I lived.

JENNY: You . . . ah . . . pointed it out to me once.

DYLAN: Oh. Ah, come in. Sorry it's such a mess . . .

JENNY: It's okay.

DYLAN: Sit down. *(They sit.)* So, ah, what's up?

JENNY: Oh, Dylan! *(She starts to cry. He stares at her.)*

DYLAN: Jenny. What's wrong? Are you okay?

JENNY: Yes . . . I'm fine.

DYLAN: What's wrong?

JENNY: Oh, I have nowhere to go. Millie's being so mean to me, and Julia and Suzanne are acting weird, and I just . . .

DYLAN: Hey, it's okay. *(He gets up.)* Can I get you anything? A drink or something? I'd offer you food, but my mom's a health food nut.

JENNY: It's okay.

DYLAN: Tea?

JENNY: No, really, don't bother. *(Calmer now, she walks around the room.)* Is all this art yours?

DYLAN: Just the sculpture. The paintings are my mom's. *(She picks up a sculpture.)* Do you like that? It took me two weeks!

JENNY: It's beautiful. (DYLAN *takes a film canister that had been under the sculpture before she picked it up. He gets out a joint.)*

DYLAN: Wanna smoke?

JENNY: Ah . . . pot?

DYLAN: Yeah.

JENNY: Oh, ah, okay. Sure, why not. *(He takes a lighter from his pocket and lights it, inhales, and passes it to her. She does the same, imitating him exactly.)*

DYLAN *(exhaling):* Feel better?

JENNY: I'm okay. *(Passes it back to him.)*

DYLAN: So, ah, how do you like this place?

JENNY: THIS place?

DYLAN: No, I mean, California. Want more?

JENNY: No thank you. *(He puts it out.)*

DYLAN: Well?

JENNY: It's okay. How do you like it?

DYLAN: I live here.

JENNY: Yeah, that's true. *(Pause.)* Can I ask you something?

DYLAN: Sure.

JENNY *(pointing to a mark on his arm):* Where did you get this?

DYLAN: What? Oh, that? I was born with it, I guess.

JENNY: Oh, you mean like a mole? It's a really big mole. Well, some people call them moles. . . . I call them beauty marks. 'Cause I have one.

DYLAN: Where?

JENNY *(pointing to a spot next to her mouth):* There. *(He moves in closer for a look.)*

DYLAN: Oh, yeah, I see it. *(He touches it, then kisses her lightly. She looks away, giggling. He pulls her face back, then they kiss again, for a longer time, and passionately. He tries to ease her dress off.)*

JENNY: Stop it! What are you doing?

DYLAN *(giggling):* I'm taking your clothes off, as far as I can see.

JENNY *(laughing):* Oh, but Dylan, I feel naked without them.

DYLAN: Oh, Jenny, sex is a cure-all. You'll never be depressed again. Come on. *(He massages her back.)*

JENNY: Do you love me?

DYLAN: Do I what?

JENNY *(singing):* Do you love me?

(He laughs.)

JENNY: Well?

DYLAN: I like your back.

(Pause. Then she jumps away.)

JENNY: No, no, wait a minute. That's not what you're supposed to say!

DYLAN: What?

JENNY: You want to sleep with me. You want to *defile my virginal innocence.*

DYLAN: What do you want, an engagement ring?

JENNY: Yes! Or some kind of commitment. I want to know you're not going to toss me off like a used condom tomorrow morning.

DYLAN: Is everyone from New York like this?

JENNY: I'm serious.

DYLAN: Take it on faith, Jenny, I like you.

JENNY: Is it unreasonable for me to want some stability in my life?

DYLAN: Is it unreasonable that I'm just not ready to commit myself to someone I've known for two weeks and who's going back to New York next week?

JENNY: But you like me. You said so.

DYLAN: I do. Why can't we just have fun while you're here?

JENNY: I need to know where I stand.

DYLAN: You stand on my living room floor. And I want to make love to you because I think it will be mutually enjoyable. It will be like sharing a piece of me with a piece of you.

JENNY: Say that again.

DYLAN: A piece of me with . . .

JENNY: No, not that. Say you want to make *love* to me.

DYLAN: I do.

JENNY: I'll tell you why you can't. Because you can't make *love* to someone you don't *love, and you don't love me, so say it the other way!*

DYLAN: What?

JENNY: *Say you want to . . . to screw me, Dylan.*

DYLAN: Is there anything wrong with that?

JENNY: *(Picks up a piece of sculpture. Pause. Then she throws it across the room.* DYLAN *screams and runs to where it fell. She picks up another.)* Still want to sleep with me, Dylan? Ever done it with a crazy woman before?

DYLAN: *Don't!*

JENNY: You're a douche bag, Dylan. And you're a real sleaze. 'Bye. *(She exits. He looks after her.)*

SCENE SEVEN

Suzanne's apartment. Early morning. SUZANNE *is asleep on the sofa, and the place is a mess. It has all the makings of a girls' night in. Pounding on the door.* SUZANNE *stirs. Louder then.*

SUZANNE: All right, all right, I'm coming. *(She picks her way to the door and opens it.* MILLIE.*)*

SUZANNE: Oh, ah, Breeze. Come in.

MILLIE: *(Enters and does a quick survey of the room.)* Is she here?

SUZANNE: Who?

MILLIE: Jenny.

SUZANNE: No, of course not. Didn't she come back to the hotel last night?

MILLIE: No! I called Dylan this morning, and he said he kicked her out after she went totally berserk and broke one of his best pieces.

SUZANNE: You mean you don't know where she is?

MILLIE: No!

SUZANNE: I guess we better wake Julia. Oh, what a thing to wake up to! *(Calls her.)* Julia!

JULIA *(Offstage):* Just another hour, okay, Suzanne?

SUZANNE: No, dear, you better come out here.

(Pause.)

MILLIE: Julia, it's important!

JULIA: Oh, all right. *(She stumbles in.)* What is it?

SUZANNE: Well, I don't know how to tell you this . . .

MILLIE: Jenny's gone.

JULIA: Gone? Where is she?

MILLIE: Gone.

SUZANNE: We don't know where she is.

(Pause.)

JULIA: She'll be back, she's very responsible. *(She starts back to bed.)*

SUZANNE: Julia, stay here.

JULIA: What time is it? *(Collapses on couch and picks up blanket.)*

SUZANNE: Nine thirty.

JULIA: She could have at least run away at a decent hour. What time is my tennis lesson?

MILLIE: Julia, I'm scared. She didn't come back to the hotel last night and she's probably running around and she's still wearing that awful dress you put her in and . . .

JULIA *(smiling):* Did you try Dylan's house?

MILLIE: *Yes, I* . . . Dylan threw her out after she went crazy and started breaking his sculpture, and she's probably stoned and crazy and wandering around Berkeley, and she was out all night, she was probably raped or—

SUZANNE: Do you want me to call the police?

JULIA: The *police*? Oh, I hate police. I'll go make coffee. *(She exits.)*

MILLIE: *(Picks up telephone and dials.)* Hello? Yes, I'd like to report a missing person. Her name is . . . uh . . . since about eleven-thirty last night . . . *twenty-four hours?* But, officer . . . all right. Thank you. *(She hangs up.)* Julia!

(JULIA comes back.)

JULIA: What now?

MILLIE: The police can't do anything for twenty-four hours. What are we going to do? I'm really scared!

JULIA: I'm sure she's all right. The police would tell you, this sort of thing happens all the time. And Berkeley is really very safe. Did you see what time my tennis lesson is?

SUZANNE: No, you can't play tennis now, we have to find Jenny.

JULIA: Look, the police just said there was nothing they could do.

MILLIE: But we've got to do *something!* She could be hurt. She could be . . . she could be lying dead in a ditch somewhere.

JULIA: That's the most ridiculous thing I've ever heard. I simply can't believe how childish you two are acting. Now, all we can do is just go on with our lives, and if she's not back by tonight, we'll call the police again. *(Silence.)* Well, I can't understand why a person can't go off by herself for a little peace and quiet without everyone acting like it's a big, major deal. *(Silence.)*

SUZANNE: Things do happen.

JULIA: Oh, honestly, Suzanne. Hand me that beer can. God, this place is such a mess. Am I the only one who can ever get anything done around here? Move, you're in my way. Stop it! You're depressing me.

MILLIE: Aren't you worried?

JULIA: I said, she'll be back.

MILLIE: What if she's dead?

JULIA: She's not dead. People don't just die like that.

MILLIE: I think you should talk to her if she gets back.

JULIA: *If?* Oh, really. Why should I talk to her? Certainly I can understand the need to get away from old mother.

MILLIE: Something is wrong with her!

JULIA: Nothing's wrong.

MILLIE: She broke Dylan's sculpture.

JULIA: You're getting upset over nothing. People break things all the time. That doesn't mean something is wrong with them.

SUZANNE: I think you should talk to her.

JULIA: Okay, I'll talk to her, just to shut you up. But all it will do is make me uncomfortable. I'm really bad at all this mothering stuff. I'm going to check on the coffee.

(She exits. A key in the door. SUZANNE *and* MILLIE *freeze.* JENNY *enters calmly.)*

MILLIE: Jenny!

JENNY: Hi, Millie, how are you?

MILLIE: Oh, Jenny, we were so worried. We called the police and everything. (JULIA *comes in.)*

JULIA: Oh, hi, Jenny. Do you want some coffee?

JENNY: Hi, Julia, how are you?

JULIA: Fine. Coffee?

JENNY: Please.

(JULIA *exits again.*)

MILLIE: I spoke to Dylan.

JENNY: Oh? How is he feeling? He was pretty upset last night, you know.

MILLIE: Where were you?

JENNY: I went to an all-night movie.

MILLIE: You had us worried sick.

JENNY: She doesn't look too sick to me.

(JULIA *reenters with a coffeepot and four cups on a tray. She puts it down and avoids looking at* JENNY.)

JULIA: Can everyone get themselves breakfast? I have a tennis lesson.

(*Pause.*)

SUZANNE: *Julia.*

JULIA: What? Want some toast?

MILLIE: Aren't you going to ask Jenny where she was?

JULIA: I trust her. (*They both glare at her.*) Oh, all right. Where were you?

JENNY (*through her teeth*): I went to an all-night movie.

JULIA: There, okay, you see? She went to an all-night movie. Did you have fun?

JENNY: *No!*

JULIA: Oh, I'm sorry to hear that. What movie was it?

(Silence.)

SUZANNE: Uh . . . Millie . . . let's go get some breakfast. Come on.

JULIA: Suzanne . . .

(She is gone. JULIA sits down and motions for JENNY to do the same. She clears her throat.)

JULIA *(forcing it):* Well, uh, Jenny . . . is something wrong?

JENNY: No, of course not, why?

JULIA: Millie said I should talk to you. She said something is wrong.

JENNY: Well, she's wrong.

JULIA: I want you to know that I am not angry at you for running away. I understand that growing girls need their space, and I respect that.

JENNY: Good.

JULIA: Well. I'm going to get ready for my tennis lesson, okay?

JENNY: Sure. *(Neither moves.)*

JULIA: Well, if there is a problem, you can always come to me, and I'll see that you get help. I know Suzanne must know of some reputable psychiatrists around here. . . .

JENNY: Around *here?*

JULIA: Oops. Well, I hadn't wanted to tell you yet, but Suzanne thinks it would be really good for me if I moved out here.

JENNY: Just like that?

JULIA: Well . . .

JENNY: What about your job?

JULIA: Suzanne said she was looking for a secretary anyway, so I figured I could do that until I found something else and—

JENNY: What about me?

JULIA: Well, you like it here, don't you?

JENNY: I don't want to live here!

JULIA: Why not? I mean, the weather is great, and you have friends already, it seems to me, and even a nice boyfriend, what's his name . . . ?

JENNY: I hate him.

JULIA: What happened?

JENNY: Nothing.

JULIA: No, tell me.

JENNY: He wanted to have sex and I didn't.

JULIA: Why not?

JENNY: He didn't even want a relationship. He just wanted all the fun with no strings.

JULIA: Well, what's wrong with that? I think it's nice to have freedom.

JENNY: Well, I think it sucks. I need some stability in my life.

JULIA: Is it fair to ask Dylan for that?

JENNY: Well, who am I supposed to ask? *You* tell *me*.

JULIA: You have a very stable life. I give you a home—

JENNY: You're about to yank it out from under me! You never even asked me if I wanted to move to California.

JULIA: It was your idea to come here in the first place.

JENNY: It was Millie's idea, and I certainly didn't expect you to like it so much you'd refuse to leave. Although I might have guessed—

JULIA: What is that supposed to mean?

JENNY: I don't know! You're always running away to some new diversion, whatever bright colors catch your eye.

JULIA: That's because I'm free, Jenny. I respect your freedom, you should—

JENNY: Well, maybe my freedom doesn't want to be respected so much.

JULIA: Jenny, I have to respect your freedom. My mother was . . . she was like a jailer. She never left me alone. That's why it's so important to me to be able to come and go as I choose, without having to answer to anyone, mother, daughter, anyone.

JENNY: If we move to California, I'll still need your attention just as much as I do at home. I'll still feel left out.

JULIA: Left out? But I'm always around.

JENNY: But you're never there! You treat my life like it's some game you can put away when you get tired of playing.

JULIA: When we move to California, I know I'll be more relaxed and have more time to spend with you.

(Pause.)

JENNY: Is that it? Is that our entire mother-daughter confrontation? Because if it is, then you can keep your freedom in California without me to tie you down at all. I'll go back to New York and live with Grandma.

JULIA: Is that really what you want? Jail?

JENNY: It's better than nothing.

JULIA: Then go. If you can't appreciate what I do for you, then I don't want you here.

JENNY: Oh, Mommy, please don't say that.

JULIA: What do you want me to say?

JENNY: I want to work this out with you.

JULIA: You want me to be my mother.

JENNY: I want you to be my mother!

JULIA: I am your mother!

JENNY: Well, I want you to act like it.

JULIA: I am acting like it! This is how *your* mother acts. What else do you suggest?

JENNY: Make some decisions for yourself. Give me a curfew, or . . . or, don't let me smoke! Little rules, like I had with Daddy.

JULIA: Wait a minute, I am being decisive. I have made a decision. Because it's one you don't like, it's invalid. You want curfews? Fine. In California you can have curfews up to your ears, for all I care.

JENNY: You're only moving out here because Suzanne told you to.

JULIA: I am perfectly capable of deciding I like it out here with my own thirty-six years and no-spring-chicken mind. Suzanne invited me out here, and I am moving out here, and you are coming with me, because you are my daughter. Me mother, you daughter. That's the way *you* want it, that's the way *you're* going to get it.

JENNY: There's a difference between being a dictator and being a mother.

JULIA: My mother certainly never found it, and she was a professional. I guess if anyone would know, she would. I don't want you to grow up like I did, I want you to be independent.

JENNY: You just want me off your back.

JULIA: You can't expect me to stop doing what I want to do for you. I have a life. You are a part of my life, but you are not my entire life.

JENNY: I'm nothing to you, am I? Forget it. I'm leaving. Can I please have some money to get home?

JULIA: You want me to give you money so that you can run away from me without listening to what I have to say? I mean, you sit here, completely ignoring me, telling me everything I want, everything I stand for, is *nothing,* and then you want money?

JENNY: Well, I have to get home.

JULIA: Home where?

JENNY: Home to Grandma.

JULIA: What if Grandma doesn't want you?

JENNY: Well, she isn't going to turn me away.

JULIA: Why don't you stay here with me, Jenny? Grandma is pretty much retired. I am your mother.

JENNY: You don't want me to stay.

JULIA: Stop putting words in my mouth! Of course I want you to stay. Do you think for a minute your father would have gone to Kenya if I hadn't wanted you to stay with me?

JENNY: Then when are *we* going back to New York?

JULIA: Oh, you're so mature, you won't even compromise a little bit.

JENNY: What do you mean?

JULIA: I told you I'd try. What do you want, a public apology? Do you want me to do penance?

JENNY: Just forget it. I'll borrow money from Millie.

JULIA: Jenny!

JENNY: What?

JULIA: Sit down and listen to me!

JENNY: I'm leaving.

JULIA: You won't listen to me! I could be mothering you, and you wouldn't even notice.

JENNY: It's too late.

JULIA: Then why did you want to discuss anything at all? If it's too late, then why is everything a big deal?

JENNY: Nothing is a big deal. I'm leaving.

JULIA: Jennifer, you sit down right now and listen to me! *(Pause. Then, JENNY sits. And she is smiling, slightly.)*

DEBRA TERRI NEFF

I'm a sophomore at Tufts University, and my academic concentration is drama and English. Originally, I'm from Queens, New York, and I went to the Saint Ann's School in Brooklyn. I know they would want to be mentioned here, so I will mention them. Hi, Saint Ann's! How are you? *Children* got its first production at Saint Ann's, at their Annual Playwriting Festival. This was a long time ago, but I still have the dress I wore to it. I think it still fits. Maybe I'll wear it again sometime.

My playwriting teacher at Saint Ann's was Nancy Fales Garrett. She was really an unbelievable amount of help and encouraged me to submit my play to the Young Playwrights Festival. So I did. My mother said, "If you win, everyone's going to think I'm just like your character Julia."

"Don't worry, Mom," I said. "I won't win."

"Well, don't get your hopes up anyway," said my father. "Although they'd be crazy not to take you. . . ." My parents: aren't they cute? They saved a bottle of champagne in the basement—just in case.

I found out I was a finalist in April, and then went to lunch with Charles Karchmer and Wendy Wasserstein. I was a great fan of Wendy's before I even entered the Young Playwrights Festival. I saw *Isn't It Romantic?* in New York, and I loved it. I decided I wanted to write just like her. So I was pretty nervous about meeting her. But it was wonderful. Wendy Wasserstein and Charles Karchmer were very nice and laced their brutally honest criticism with a lot of praise, and they even bought me lunch. So then I did a few minor revisions, usually during rehearsals, and I did a few major revisions, including completely reversing the ending.

I don't remember what revisions I did when; I only remember there were a lot of them, and they were often frustrating. I hadn't looked at the play in a few months, and some problems became obvious when I looked at it again. I did my best to fix them. Charles and Wendy were very helpful and encouraged me not to take their advice, although I often did. By the time my reading took place, I was so sick of *Children*. I had just completed a new play and wanted to concentrate on that. I flew home from school for the reading, which went very well. I particularly liked the casting choice of Leslie Lyles as Julia. Then I put *Children* away and did not look at it again until this summer, when I had to edit out all the cuss words for publication.

All that time, I was not sure about the changed ending, but I left it in, because everyone else seemed to like it so much. I look at the play now, and I like the new ending better. Now I see what the play is really all about and why the new ending is more successful. When I wrote the play I didn't think, "Gee, I think for my first play I'll do a study of the generation of women who reject their mothers' values and try to raise their children in the laissez-faire manner in which they themselves would like to have been reared." I was just sort of playing. But I see that the point of view in the original version was one-sided. All I could see was how Jenny was right. I had friends like her who had mothers like Julia, and I sympathized with my friends, although it did seem like a neat kind of mother to have. Charles Karchmer and Wendy Wasserstein saw immediately what I had done and pointed it out to me. From there it was a great effort to see Julia's point of view, to try to figure out how this woman would reconcile her anger at her mother with her love for her daughter. I think the new ending shows Julia making a compromise that the audience can respect her for and she can respect herself for.

Right now I am working on a third play. I'm finding it very easy to get distance from it, since here at Tufts there are so many distractions.

I was able to put my second play on at Tufts last year, and hope to present my new one here as well (if I ever finish it). I plan to study in England next year, and then I don't know. I know that I want to keep writing plays and having them produced, and I think that's the only thing I know I want to be doing in five, ten, twenty, fifty years.

SENIORITY

by Eric Ziegenhagen
(age sixteen when play was written)
St. Paul, Minnesota

NOTE:
For the purpose of publication in this collection, certain words
have been changed by the playwright, and some profanity has been
deleted from the working script of the play as performed at Playwrights Horizons, New York City, September 13 through October
8, 1988.

Seniority was first performed at Playwrights Horizons on September 13, 1988. The director was Lisa Peterson. The playwright adviser was Alfred Uhry. The cast:

DEBBIE, *seventeen, a senior in high*
  school . . . . Bellina Logan
FIONA, *her sister, almost fifteen,*
  a freshman in high school . . . . Allison Dean
IAN, *a senior in high school* . . . . Jihmi Kennedy

SETTING:
The living room of a house in a suburb.

TIME:
Autumn. Midnight.

SCENE:
A card table with pamphlets on it. There is also a staircase, a folding chair or two, and a floor lamp. Light comes from the lamp, except for some moonlight and streetlights from outside.

DEBBIE *is paging through a pamphlet. Offstage, a teakettle blows.* DEBBIE *exits to kitchen and comes back with a cup in her hands. A car is heard outside.* DEBBIE *exits to kitchen again. The car idles and then pulls away.* DEBBIE *reenters carrying another cup and the kettle. As* FIONA *enters,* DEBBIE *pours two cups of tea.)*

FIONA: Hi.

DEBBIE: 'Morning.

FIONA: You're still up. It's late, isn't it?

DEBBIE: Midnight.

FIONA: Oh. I didn't wear my watch.

DEBBIE: I made you some tea.

FIONA: Thank you.

DEBBIE: Just was making some and figured you'd be back soon, so I made a little extra.

FIONA: Thank you.

DEBBIE: Dawn called for you tonight.

FIONA: What did you tell her?

DEBBIE: I said that you were going to be out late.

FIONA: She didn't ask where I was?

DEBBIE: She just wanted to know if you wanted to do something tomorrow.

FIONA: Did she ask where I was?

DEBBIE: No. I told her you were out.

FIONA: Good.

DEBBIE: So how was it?

FIONA: Fun. Really fun. What happened in here?

DEBBIE: What?

FIONA: All this mess.

DEBBIE: Bridge game. Grandmother Jessica's staying here. There's a bridge tournament at the Holiday Inn.

FIONA: Then why is this stuff here?

DEBBIE: She had some of her friends over.

FIONA: Why don't they just play over at the Holiday Inn if she's staying over there?

DEBBIE: The tournament's there, but she's staying upstairs. She's sleeping in the TV room. Don't worry about it, anyway, you won't have to clean it up. I'll take care of it.

FIONA *(noticing pamphlets):* What are these?

DEBBIE: Pamphlets I picked up today. European exchanges. Two weeks in Holland, two weeks in England. Room and board at universities in London and Amsterdam. Seventeen hundred dollars including everything except extra spending. There's time to study and time to tour. Four weeks to get away. Exactly the sort of thing I'm looking for.

FIONA: You were thinking of doing this alone?

DEBBIE: No. With a study group. Well, "alone" meaning not being with anyone I know, yeah, I guess.

FIONA: And you think Mom will let you do that?

DEBBIE: Yes, I do.

FIONA: I beg to differ.

DEBBIE: Oh. We'll see. If I'm going to be going away to college next year, I don't see why she wouldn't let me spend a few weeks by myself in Europe.

FIONA: Because it's dangerous, Debbie. Dangerous. I mean, Amsterdam . . . it's, it's heroin and hookers . . . guys in ugly trench coats who want to feed you sourdough bread with poison in it . . . get your purse stolen, bad rates on money exchange . . .

DEBBIE: I'd be careful. I'd know where not to walk.

FIONA: It's too dangerous, Debbie. She'll never let you go.

DEBBIE: Then where could I go that wouldn't be dangerous? Omaha? I could be an exchange student in Omaha, and then it would be okay?

FIONA: I didn't mean to start an argument, Debbie.

DEBBIE: It won't hurt to bring it up with Mom.

FIONA: True.

DEBBIE: I'm responsible and careful enough for it.

(Pause.)

DEBBIE: Does Mom know that you went out tonight?

FIONA: She knew that I went out . . .

DEBBIE: . . . but not with a guy.

FIONA: Right. You didn't say anything, did you?

DEBBIE: No, but didn't he come in when he picked you up?

FIONA: No.

DEBBIE: You just went out there and met him?

FIONA: Yeah. Is there something wrong—

DEBBIE: No, no, it's just whenever I've gone out on dates, it's always kind of cute and romantic to meet the parents. You know, he would always go in and shake hands with Mom or whatever when he picked me up.

FIONA: Why should a guy have to go through that trouble when Mom probably won't like him anyway?

DEBBIE: It's kind of a custom.

FIONA: And that's what you've done on dates.

DEBBIE: Yeah, I've done that. Once we even went into the house after going out to a movie and, well, all right, we didn't expect his parents to be home, but his mom made some cocoa, and we all stayed up late just talking. The three of us. It wasn't bad at all.

FIONA: When was this?

DEBBIE: Last year.

FIONA: When did you go out?

DEBBIE: I went to prom, Fiona, remember? I also went out a few times this summer.

FIONA: I don't remember that.

DEBBIE: It was while you were out in Phoenix visiting Dad, that's why.

FIONA: Oh, I see.

DEBBIE: So where did you go?

FIONA: We just went out to the mall and walked around and ate some dinner.

DEBBIE: You ate in the mall?

FIONA: That fifties place over by the movie theater. It has those pink neon . . .

DEBBIE *(overlapping):* Yeah, I know what you're talking about.

FIONA: . . . lights in the window and an old Wurlitzer jukebox. The kind with little water bubbles going up the sides in different colors.

DEBBIE: Yeah.

FIONA: Real cute.

DEBBIE: Yeah.

FIONA: And then after that we went to a movie.

DEBBIE: At the mall?

FIONA: Yeah, where else would you go?

DEBBIE: What did you see?

FIONA: What?

DEBBIE: What was the movie?

FIONA: Boring. Something real boring. Some horror movie. Didn't watch it much.

DEBBIE: Oh.

FIONA: So that's about it.

DEBBIE: That leaves about three hours to spare.

FIONA: You don't have to clock my every moment, Debbie.

DEBBIE: Just curious, that's all.

FIONA: We drove around a little.
  Went out around the outskirts of town.
  You know, you can't see many stars around here, but way out on Highway Nineteen, past the suburbs and into the country, there were so many stars, I couldn't believe it. Not just the Big Dipper. Ones you can't see from here. And it's such a beautiful night out. Not too chilly. A thin, cool wind. Crickets.
  We just laid in some field by the side of the road, breathing the air and watching the stars. It was romantic and fun. What else is a date supposed to be?

DEBBIE: You did it, didn't you?

FIONA: We just went out, Debbie. A date.

DEBBIE: I knew I could see something even when you came in here. You're light.

FIONA: I can't be happy?

DEBBIE: You're more than happy . . .

FIONA: Sure we kissed, but—

DEBBIE: More than that. I can see it, Fiona. You're transparent.

FIONA: You're wrong.

DEBBIE: Right through you.

FIONA: Debbie.

(Long pause.)

FIONA: And so what if I did? So what if I "did it"? What then? You're just jealous, Debbie. You wish that you were in my place. Not with him, maybe, but with anyone. Anyone under the stars.

DEBBIE: That's not true!

FIONA: Anyone that would offer it!

DEBBIE: I've had the—

FIONA: But no one asks you, so you just wait and wait and wait, and now you're jealous. I can read you, too. You envy me because I had a chance that you never did.

DEBBIE: I've had the opportunity, Fiona. I just didn't take it. It wasn't like he was so sure about it either.

FIONA *(overlapping):* Who?

DEBBIE: He asked if it would seem right and I said that it wouldn't.

FIONA *(overlapping):* Who?

DEBBIE: And it didn't seem right. It was that simple. And he understood. He gave me a choice.

FIONA: I didn't do it against my will . . .

DEBBIE: I know.

FIONA: . . . we wanted to and we did.

DEBBIE: And when you miss your period next month and end up with a little embryo inside of you, you'll know something about taking chances.

FIONA: We were careful.

DEBBIE: But let's say something went wrong and something happened to sneak inside you and you get pregnant. Then you'll be a mommy. And our mother will be a grandma. And this man, this *guy,* this guy whose middle name you probably don't even know, will be the father. And you'll both have to take care . . .

FIONA *(overlapping):* We were careful.

DEBBIE: . . . of it for the next eighteen years.

FIONA: There would always be abortion or adoption or something. Anyway, I'm not pregnant.

DEBBIE: How can you be sure?

FIONA: We were careful.

DEBBIE: The point is . . . Fiona, the point is *responsibility.* I don't think you're responsible enough—

FIONA: We were responsible enough to be careful, so I don't care how you feel about it. It's none of your business.

(Pause.)

DEBBIE: You want some more tea?

FIONA: No thanks.

DEBBIE: Sure?

FIONA: I haven't even drunk what I have now.

DEBBIE: If you didn't want any, you should've told me.

FIONA: It's all right.

(DEBBIE pours a cup for herself.)

DEBBIE: So, what do you see in this guy, anyway?

FIONA: What?

DEBBIE: What's so special about him?

FIONA: He's nice.

DEBBIE: What's special?

FIONA: I like him.

DEBBIE: But what does he have that makes him the one? The right one for you?

(Pause.)

FIONA: I don't know.

DEBBIE: Anything at all? Anything recognizable in him? Is he smart? Is he funny? Does he have a cute ass?

FIONA: Yes. He does. And he's really sweet. Kind of funny.

DEBBIE: He's "kind of funny." That's all?

FIONA: He's a human being. I like him and he likes me.

DEBBIE: And what if he's just using you?

FIONA: He's not.

DEBBIE: How do you know this? *(Pause.)* Look, Fiona, I just don't want some guy to . . . I was in ninth grade once. I know how girls are in ninth grade. I don't want some guy taking advantage of your curiosity.

FIONA: We both wanted to. Nobody was taking advantage of anyone. We like each other. We get along well together. We both wanted to do it and we did it. We don't regret it. We both enjoyed it.

DEBBIE: You really enjoyed it?

FIONA: Yes, Debbie, I did.

DEBBIE: It's just they say you don't enjoy the first time.

FIONA: It was romance. It was being with someone. Just being with someone under the stars and enjoying it.

DEBBIE: But didn't it—

FIONA: You ever sit outside, watching the sun rise or set or watching some really funny movie all alone and say to yourself, "God, I wish I had someone to share this with"? Well, that's the kind of night it was, and the best thing of all was that I was sharing it with somebody.

DEBBIE: Who is he?

FIONA: I was embarrassed to tell you before and . . . and I can't tell you *now*.

DEBBIE: I don't spread gossip.

FIONA: I know. I just can't tell.

DEBBIE: I'll probably end up hearing it on Monday at school from his friends.

FIONA: We promised not to tell anyone.

DEBBIE: You've told me everything else. I need to know.

(Pause.)

FIONA: I'll probably go out with him again, so you might as well know. *(Pause.)* Except that you don't know him.

DEBBIE: Come on, I know a lot of freshmen.

FIONA: Well, I don't think you know him.

DEBBIE: Then what's his name?

FIONA: Ian.

DEBBIE: Ian?

FIONA: Yes.

DEBBIE: I don't know any freshmen named Ian.

FIONA: I didn't think so.

DEBBIE: I don't think there are any freshmen named Ian.

(Pause.)

DEBBIE: Ian Weston?

(Pause.)

FIONA: Yes.

DEBBIE: He's in *my* grade, Fiona! He's a *senior!* He's, what is he, seventeen, eighteen—

FIONA: He'll be eighteen tomorrow.

DEBBIE: His birthday's tomorrow?

FIONA: It's after midnight now. Tomorrow's today, so now it's his birthday. I got him a card.

DEBBIE: He's three years older than you are!

FIONA: I don't care, and neither does he.

DEBBIE: You ought to.

FIONA: Why? It's not that big of an age difference. Look at movie stars. Sixty-year-old actors marrying twenty-year-old models, now that is a big difference. But, look, we really aren't that far apart.

DEBBIE: But there's that sense of discovery—

FIONA: He hasn't gone out with many girls. Was he at prom last year?

DEBBIE: I don't remember. I don't think so.

(Pause. DEBBIE *goes to the stairs.)*

FIONA: Going to bed?

DEBBIE: No. I'll be back in a minute.

*(*FIONA *picks up a pamphlet and looks through it.* DEBBIE *goes upstairs. As* FIONA *speaks,* DEBBIE *comes back down the staircase with a yearbook open in her hands.)*

FIONA: Why do you want to go away in the first place? Can't you wait and do that in college?

DEBBIE: "Debbie, It's been great knowing you this year. Algebra was boring, but we sure had fun. Have a nice summer. Signed, Ian." That's all he wrote. Unoriginal bastard. No sincerity at all.

FIONA: Just because he writes, "Have a nice summer," in your yearbook doesn't mean he's insensitive. Everyone writes, "Have a nice summer," in everyone's yearbook.

DEBBIE: But I've known him. I've talked to him. He ought to have written something nicer in my yearbook. I did in his.

FIONA: What did you write?

DEBBIE: Just that . . . just . . . I don't remember.

FIONA: What did you write?

DEBBIE: I don't remember the exact phrasing . . .

FIONA: What was it?

DEBBIE: I . . . I just wrote that I was going to miss him in a year when we graduate.

FIONA: You liked him?

DEBBIE: I'm going to miss a lot of people.

FIONA: But you liked this guy.

DEBBIE: Yes. I did.

(Pause.)

FIONA: I'm sorry, Debbie.

DEBBIE: I liked him until I realized how shallow he was.

FIONA: What makes you think he's shallow?

DEBBIE: Look, Fiona. Two years ago I really liked him. I wanted to go out with him. I talked to him whenever I got the chance to in school. And I liked him, yes, but then for a while we didn't talk. There was a semester when we didn't have any classes together. And then, as I started seeing less and less of him, I began realizing what I liked about him was what he could be, what he was in my mind. I was distanced from him, so I could create who he was in my mind. He became almost more than human to me. He was like a custom-made guy for me because I made him out to be anything that I wanted to. He had the perfect personality because I didn't know his true one. When you're distanced, you lie to yourself. You lie to yourself and rationalize the rest. I was just looking at a shadow from the past. That's all.

(Pause.)

FIONA: So, since he's not perfect, he's shallow?

DEBBIE: That wasn't my point, I was trying to—

FIONA: But you said he was shallow.

DEBBIE: That's what some of my friends who know him better than I do say.

FIONA: He doesn't seem shallow to—

DEBBIE: How long have you known him, Fiona?

FIONA: Couple weeks. He works in the art room during my art class sometimes.

DEBBIE *(overlapping):* But if you—

FIONA: It's his free hour and he likes to go there and paint. I talk to him a lot.

DEBBIE: I've known him for a long time, and he really doesn't seem like that deep of—

FIONA: Maybe you've just watched him from a distance for a long, long time, and now that you realize that you can't have him, you're making him out to be a real shallow guy, just to, well, "cut your losses," you know.

DEBBIE: Maybe I am.

FIONA: I don't want to be competing against you.

DEBBIE: You aren't.

FIONA: I am. You like this guy.

DEBBIE: I liked him. There are other guys, Fiona.

FIONA: But when's the last time you went on a date?

DEBBIE: I've never gone out with Ian.

FIONA: I meant with anyone.

(Pause.)

DEBBIE: I don't know.

FIONA: You don't?

DEBBIE: Okay, it was July. Went to a concert.

FIONA: So, don't you want to go out with some guy?

DEBBIE: Yeah, it just doesn't seem to work. Doesn't fall into place like it should. Either I know the guy too well, or I don't know him well enough, or . . . I don't know . . . I can't deal with it.

FIONA: Debbie, you could find a date. You can even drive.

DEBBIE: It's not easy to get your nerve up.

FIONA: I know.

DEBBIE: How do you know, Fiona? How do you know? You don't know what it's like to have to ask someone out.

FIONA: I asked Ian out.

(Pause.)

DEBBIE: You said before that he—

FIONA: No, I didn't.

DEBBIE: I guess I was assuming.

FIONA: He wouldn't've asked me out if I hadn't asked him.

DEBBIE: The guy is supposed to ask out the girl.

FIONA: Then you're going to be spending a lot of evenings waiting by the phone, Debbie.

DEBBIE: Just because you get some guy—

FIONA: I didn't mean it personally. I mean that it's as hard for the guy to ask you out as it is for you.

DEBBIE: But if a guy really wanted to go out with me, he'd be able to ask me out.

FIONA: When you liked Ian, did you ask him out?

DEBBIE: It's easier for the guy—

FIONA: Debbie, it isn't. The sooner you realize that it's just as hard, the sooner you'll get a date.

DEBBIE: I don't want to go out with a guy if he doesn't want to go out with me, and if he wants to go out with me, he can get the nerve to ask me.

FIONA: Who doesn't like a date? Why *wouldn't* a guy want to go out with you?

DEBBIE: I'm not pretty.

FIONA: You aren't ugly, so that's no excuse.

DEBBIE: Pretty guys have pretty girlfriends already.

FIONA: Not all of them.

DEBBIE: They do.

FIONA: I'm not any prettier than you are, and I went out—

DEBBIE: I don't know why.

FIONA: Because I wanted to and I had the guts to ask him out. *(Pause.)* And I'm not any prettier than you are. I'm just a fourteen-year-old.

DEBBIE: You're "cute," though.

FIONA: Having not much of a chest and too much acne is not "cute."

DEBBIE: You have one pimple on your face and you want to be quarantined.

FIONA: I'm careful of how I look. That's why I'm confident.

DEBBIE: Are you saying that I'm not—

FIONA: No. It's better for you to look . . . well, I don't mean to insult you.

DEBBIE: What?

FIONA: Well, to look kind of plain. I mean, it's better to look like that than put on too much eye shadow and wear tight red pants.

DEBBIE: Am I plain?

FIONA: No. I just can't think of a better word. You just don't try to stick out in the crowd.

DEBBIE: Plain.

FIONA: No. I'm sorry I used that word.

DEBBIE: Is it what you meant?

FIONA: No.

DEBBIE: Be honest.

FIONA: No. You're pretty, Debbie.

DEBBIE: Then why can't I get a boyfriend?

FIONA: Just ask someone out. Anyone. Take a chance. If I could go out with a senior just by asking him, you could go out with anyone.

DEBBIE: Not if I can't ask him.

FIONA: Try.

DEBBIE: I just can't ask guys out. I'm . . . I just can't.

FIONA: Then what can I do to help you?

DEBBIE: I don't need help, I just need . . .

FIONA: . . . a boyfriend.

(Pause.)

DEBBIE: It's really patronizing for you to give me all this advice, you know.

FIONA: I'm just trying to help you.

DEBBIE: I . . . I don't know.

FIONA: Just pick out a guy and call him up.

DEBBIE: What do I say?

FIONA: Just be honest.

DEBBIE: If I don't have anything to say . . .

FIONA: Then maybe he's the wrong guy. Are there any guys who you can talk to?

(Pause.)

DEBBIE: I just get nervous and dumb.

FIONA: You aren't nervous and dumb, though.

DEBBIE: You haven't seen me with guys.

FIONA: You just need to meet some guys.

DEBBIE: I know, Fiona.

(Pause.)

DEBBIE: I just don't know what to do.

(Pause.)

FIONA: Look, Deb, no one's going to call you up tonight, so you might as well just go to sleep. You get depressed when you're tired.

DEBBIE: I couldn't get to sleep before. That's why I made some tea.

FIONA: Well, it's pretty late. Are you coming up or should I leave the light on?

DEBBIE: I don't feel tired.

(Pause.)

FIONA: You know, Debbie, I think you've just got some deep scar inside you that you're gonna dig up sometime and wonder what you've been missing. *(She goes up the stairs.)* I'll see you in the morning.

DEBBIE: I hope you don't wake up tomorrow crying and regretting what you've done tonight.

FIONA: Good night.

DEBBIE: Little girl.

(DEBBIE picks up teapot and cups and exits, then reenters without them. She turns off the lamp. Moonlight and suburban streetlights light the room. She is going up the stairs when there is a quiet knock on the front door and then another. She turns the lamp back on and goes to the door. IAN enters, carrying a small purse.)

IAN: Hi, Debbie.

DEBBIE: Ian. Hello.

IAN *(indicating purse):* Fiona left this in my car.

DEBBIE: She's gone to bed.

IAN: Do you think she's awake?

DEBBIE: No.

IAN: Could I go up and see?

DEBBIE: She doesn't like being waked up.

IAN: She won't mind it. *(He crosses to staircase.)*

DEBBIE: No. Don't go up there. *(Pause.)* Please. You'll wake my mother up. She's a light sleeper.

IAN: I'll be quiet.

DEBBIE: My grandmother's staying up there.

IAN: It'll be okay.

DEBBIE: Both Fiona and I will be in a lot of trouble if my mother wakes up, some guy prowling around her upstairs. . . . Fiona would get grounded. So would I. You wouldn't be able to talk to her except in school.

IAN: Do you have anything to drink?

DEBBIE: Why don't you just leave the purse down here?

IAN: I'm really thirsty.

(Pause.)

DEBBIE: Water?

IAN: Sure.

(DEBBIE exits. IAN sets the purse on the table. A moment later DEBBIE reenters with a glass of water.)

DEBBIE: How was your date?

IAN: It went really well. *(Takes glass.)* Thanks.

DEBBIE: Fiona seemed ready to fall right into the sack when she got home. You don't seem very tired.

IAN: I'm used to staying up late.

DEBBIE: But she was really *exhausted.*

IAN: Dates do that to you sometimes.

DEBBIE: Do you think you two'll go out again?

IAN: I'd like to if she wants to.

DEBBIE: That's good. *(Pause.)* Good movie?

IAN: I liked it. Fiona didn't seem to.

DEBBIE: What did you see?

IAN: *Poltergeist Three.* It was really pretty bad, actually.

DEBBIE: Fiona said it was boring.

IAN: It was.

DEBBIE: But you had a good time.

IAN: Yes. How was your evening?

DEBBIE: My evening?

IAN: Yes.

DEBBIE: Oh, I don't know. It wasn't very interesting. I've just been doing some reading, watching television, you know, that stuff.

IAN: What are you reading?

DEBBIE: Well . . . just this science fiction book that I got for last summer. Finally am getting around to reading it.

IAN: What is it?

DEBBIE: It's really dumb, that's what it is . . . ah . . . *The Valley of Time.*

IAN: Is it good?

DEBBIE: I guess.

IAN: How did you do on the Spanish test?

DEBBIE: I got a B.

IAN: Not bad. A lot of people did worse.

(Pause.)

DEBBIE: How did you do?

IAN: On the Spanish test?

DEBBIE: Yeah.

IAN: B minus.

DEBBIE: That's not bad.

IAN: It's what I expected.

(Pause.)

DEBBIE: Are you hungry at all?

IAN: Not really. Thanks for offering.

DEBBIE: Are you going to the dance next Friday?

IAN: I was actually thinking of asking Fiona.

DEBBIE: Be gentle with her.

IAN: I don't understand.

DEBBIE: Oh, you know, she's my little sister and all. I keep telling her to be careful.

IAN: Don't worry about it.

DEBBIE: I do, though. You know, just 'cause she's a freshman and all . . .

IAN: She's very mature, though.

DEBBIE: It's strange to think of you going out with my little sister.

IAN: I was worried about what you'd think.

DEBBIE: I think I'll be all right.

IAN: There's really nothing to worry about. She's mature for her age.

DEBBIE: I don't know . . . it's just that I really . . . I don't know.

IAN: What?

DEBBIE: I'm . . . I don't know . . . she . . . sometimes I wish I had the chance to go out when, back when I was a freshman, but then I think that it's for the better, but then . . . I . . . I don't know . . . I don't know if I'm right . . . I'm, I'm worried about her, but I still wish . . . I don't know.

IAN: Are you going out with anyone now?

DEBBIE: No.

IAN: That's too bad. I hope you find someone.

(Long pause.)

DEBBIE: I really wanted to go out with you when we were sophomores.

IAN: I could tell. I kind of wanted to ask you out, too.

DEBBIE: But . . .

IAN: But . . . well . . . that's history.

DEBBIE: I guess so.

IAN: Yeah. I don't know. *(Pause. FIONA appears at the top of the staircase, unnoticed by IAN and DEBBIE.)* You know what's wild, though? I had this dream about the two of you once. You both were in it. It wasn't dirty or anything. We were sitting at this white wire table in white wire chairs in the middle of this gazebo on the top of a big green hill. One of you was pouring wine, and one of you was feeding me grapes. A glass in my hand, a grape in my mouth. I just kept drinking the wine and eating the grapes, and you both had this big smile on your face like it was the time of your life. The strange thing is, I don't remember which one of you did what. The both of you were there, and we were having this meal together.

FIONA: Morning.

(IAN and DEBBIE notice FIONA.)

IAN: Hi.

DEBBIE: I thought you went to bed.

IAN: You forgot your purse.

FIONA: I know. *(Pause. To IAN):* Come upstairs.

DEBBIE: You'll wake Mom up. You'll wake Grandma up.

(Pause.)

FIONA: It's strange. It really doesn't matter to me.

(IAN crosses to stairs and ascends them, joining FIONA. They disappear above. DEBBIE takes a seat at the table and notices something inside the purse. She pulls out an unsealed envelope. She pulls a birthday card out of the envelope. She reads the cover and then opens it up. It is a card with a computer chip inside that plays "Happy Birthday." The computerized song plays as lights fade slowly to black.)

ERIC ZIEGENHAGEN

I was born in 1970 in suburban Minneapolis, where I lived for twelve years before moving a few miles away to St. Paul. I began attending Kenyon College in January 1989.

When I was eleven or twelve I took some acting classes at a community theater, where we spent all of our time running around and doing improvisational exercises, which meant that we spontaneously created the characters, situations, and words ourselves. I also took acting classes in high school, where, again, we mostly learned the fundamentals of acting through improvisation. Those experiences, combined with short-story writing and the support of the Playwrights Center, a Minneapolis organization that sponsors a Young Playwrights program, led me to playwriting.

I plan to continue to write. I can't dwell on future writing too closely because I don't know what my ideas will be or when I will get them. I just don't want to limit my studies and experiences too much at my age, out of fear that, by the time I turn twenty, I'll end up with a nice sense of structure and nothing to write about.

ABOUT THE PRODUCTION

What kept returning to my mind while in New York were thoughts I had had of a friend of mine who graduated from high school and spent the following year in Europe. She spent a few months with a family in Spain and then bopped from country to country with a Eurailpass. I had received a postcard with a picture of Amsterdam and a postmark from Bonn and thought, "How do you top this? After spending an entire year traveling around Europe at age eighteen, what's left?"

It didn't go fast and it didn't go slow, even if it was one of the most exciting times of my life; it went like any seven weeks go, except that it was full of new people, new streets, famous people, and famous streets. New York contains some of the most famous proper nouns in the world, and having this play produced at the Festival meant seeing them all shrunk down to life size. Walking through Times Square every day to get to the theater made it seem less of a world-famous tourist attraction. I went to see *The Road to Mecca* one night and ran into Athol Fugard on the street afterward. I shook his hand, gave him a compliment, and we parted. Someone on the back of a book cover somewhere called him the greatest living playwright, and he was on this streetcorner, and he was less than seven feet tall.

ABOUT THE PLAY

I have now seen this play read or performed by four different sets of actors. The script has few stage directions, so that certain choices are left to the actors and the director. Each ensemble has created an original chemistry. I've seen this play done as a light comedy and as a dark melodrama; the Festival production ended up being somewhere between the two, evenly mixing the humor and the sadness.

The characters are products of a bedroom community. They are tethered by their environment. They have nowhere to go but to the shopping mall. They are left alone to find their own values. They find romance in the idea of escape.

WOMEN AND WALLACE

by Jonathan Marc Sherman
(age eighteen when play was written)
Livingston, New Jersey

NOTE:
For the purpose of publication in this collection, certain words
have been changed by the playwright, and some profanity has been
deleted from the working script of the play as performed at Playwrights Horizons, New York City, September 13 through October
8, 1988.

Women and Wallace was first performed at Playwrights Horizons on September 13, 1988. The director was Don Scardino. Playwright adviser was Albert Innaurato. The cast:

WALLACE KIRKMAN	Josh Hamilton
MOTHER	Mary Joy
GRANDMOTHER	Joan Copeland
VICTORIA	Dana Behr
PSYCHIATRIST	Debra Monk
SARAH	Bellina Logan
LILI	Jill Tasker
NINA	Joanna Going
WENDY	Erica Gimpel

TIME:
1975 to 1987.

"The great question that has never been answered, and which I had not been able to answer, despite my thirty years of research into the feminine soul, is: What does a woman want?"—Sigmund Freud

For Maria, who justifies romance.

PROLOGUE

WALLACE *is standing to the left with a tomato in his hand and a crate of tomatoes at his feet.* NINA *is standing to the right, wearing a white dress. Pause.* WALLACE *lobs the tomato. It splatters on Nina's dress. Pause.*

WALLACE: I love you.

(Pause.)

SCENE ONE

WALLACE: "Mommy." By Wallace Kirkman. Age Six. I love Mommy because she makes me peanut butter and banana sandwiches on Wonder bread and it tastes better than when I order it at a restaurant. And Mommy never looks at me funny like the waiters in restaurants do. And Mommy crushes aspirins and mixes them into jelly when I get sick. Because I can't swallow aspirins. They just sit on my tongue and wait for me to finish the whole glass of water. And then I spit them out. But when they're mixed into jelly, I hardly have any problem at all. I just eat the jelly and feel better. And Mommy washes my clothes, so I don't have to. And she does it so they all smell nice when they come out. They come out smelling clean. And they even smell a little like Mommy, because she folds them for me, and her smell rubs off onto my shirts. She smells like perfume. Not really sweet, like Billy Corkscrew's mother. Mommy smells like she's getting ready to go out to dinner. And Mommy's read every book in the library downstairs. I couldn't do that. She can read three books in a week with no trouble at all. Real books, not the Hardy Boys. Mommy's really smart. She can read and take care of me. Both. That's why I love Mommy.

SCENE TWO

The kitchen. MOTHER *is fixing a peanut butter and banana sandwich with a large knife. She puts it into a lunchbox on the table.* WALLACE *runs in.*

WALLACE: I'm going to miss the bus! Is my lunch ready?

MOTHER: All set.

(WALLACE *grabs the lunchbox and kisses* MOTHER *on the cheek.*)

WALLACE: 'Bye, Mommy.

MOTHER: 'Bye, Wallace.

WALLACE *(to the audience)*: I love the second grade!

MOTHER: Don't shout, Wallace.

(WALLACE *runs out.* MOTHER *watches after him. She writes a note on a slip of paper and puts it on the table. She takes off her turtleneck shirt, so she is in her brassiere. She slits her throat with the large knife. She falls to the floor. Pause.* WALLACE *runs in.*)

WALLACE: Mommy, I'm home! (WALLACE *sees* MOTHER *on the floor. He picks up the note.*)

WALLACE *(reading the note)*: "Cremate the parasite."

SCENE THREE

Wallace's bedroom. WALLACE *is lying on his bed.* GRANDMOTHER *walks in, holding a gift and a photograph.*

GRANDMOTHER: Here you are. Your teacher gave me this gift for you.

WALLACE: It's not my birthday.

GRANDMOTHER: Well, something bad happened to you. When something bad happens, you get gifts to make you feel better.

WALLACE: Why do I get gifts on my birthday?

GRANDMOTHER: Well, because you're a year older.

WALLACE: Being a year older isn't bad.

GRANDMOTHER: It adds up. Open your gift.

(WALLACE *opens his gift.*)

WALLACE: Peanut brittle.

GRANDMOTHER: Isn't that *lovely*—

WALLACE: I *hate* peanut brittle.

GRANDMOTHER: So do I. Don't forget to send your teacher a thank-you note.

WALLACE: Why should I *send* her something? I see her every day.

GRANDMOTHER: So *give* her a thank-you note.

WALLACE: But I *hate* peanut brittle.

GRANDMOTHER: So throw it at her during the pledge of allegiance. Just give her *something* in return for her gift. It's good manners.

WALLACE: Okay.

GRANDMOTHER: She's a very pretty woman.

WALLACE: I guess so.

GRANDMOTHER: Why aren't you downstairs?

WALLACE: Too many people. Why'd they all come back home with us?

GRANDMOTHER: I don't know. They didn't get enough grief out, maybe.

WALLACE: I think they just like free food.

GRANDMOTHER: You're probably right. They're all bunched together like a big black cloud of perfume and cologne, munching on little corned beef sandwiches. *Horrible.*

WALLACE: What's that?

GRANDMOTHER: What? *This?*

WALLACE: Yeah.

GRANDMOTHER: Oh, it's a photograph of your mother. The last one, as far as I know. Your father took it six days ago. I wanted to have it.

WALLACE: I wish Mommy would come back.

GRANDMOTHER: I know, Wallace, but for whatever reasons, she wanted to go—

WALLACE: She didn't want to.

GRANDMOTHER: What? Wallace—

WALLACE: I know she didn't want to, Grandma, I know. A pirate came in while I was at school and tore her open. He took everything inside of her and put it in his sack and escaped through the kitchen door. She didn't want to go, Grandma. And if I was here— if I pretended I was sick and stayed home—I could have saved her—

GRANDMOTHER: No. You couldn't have. Don't think you could have saved her, because I'm telling you, you couldn't have. Nobody could have. It was time for her to go. It'll be time for me to go soon, too. And someday, it'll be your time to go—

WALLACE: Not me. I'm going to live forever.

GRANDMOTHER: I wish you luck. You'd be the first person to do it.

WALLACE: I'm going to.

GRANDMOTHER: If anybody can, Wallace, I'm sure it'll be you.

WALLACE: And I'm going to find the pirate who did this. You wait and see.

GRANDMOTHER: I will, Wallace. I certainly will. *(Pause.)* You look very handsome in your suit.

WALLACE: Thank you.

SCENE FOUR

The schoolyard. WALLACE *is sitting on a bench eating a sandwich.*
VICTORIA *walks in.*

VICTORIA: Hi, Wallace.

WALLACE: Hi, Victoria.

VICTORIA: Can I sit down?

WALLACE: Free country.

(VICTORIA *sits down next to* WALLACE.)

VICTORIA: What you got for lunch?

WALLACE: Peanut butter and banana.

VICTORIA: Want to trade?

WALLACE: What do you have?

VICTORIA: Tuna.

WALLACE: No, thanks. Besides, I already ate some of mine.

VICTORIA: Peanut butter and banana's my favorite. Bet it's good.

WALLACE: It kind of sucks. My dad made it. Dads can't make
lunch. You can barely *taste* the banana.

VICTORIA: *(Pause.)* I'm sorry about your mother.

WALLACE: Yeah. Me, too.

VICTORIA: She killed herself?

WALLACE: Who told you that?

VICTORIA: I don't know. Somebody.

WALLACE: She didn't kill herself. A pirate slit her throat, I think. I haven't finished checking things out yet.

VICTORIA: Uh-uh. That's not what they said. They said, "Suicide."

WALLACE: Who cares?

VICTORIA: I don't know. *(Pause.)* You want a hug?

WALLACE *(quiet)*: Yeah.

(VICTORIA *hugs* WALLACE *for a few moments. He pushes her away suddenly, and she falls.*)

WALLACE: Get away from me! *(Pause.)* I gotta go.

(WALLACE *runs out. Pause.* VICTORIA *walks over to* WALLACE'S *sandwich and looks at it. She picks it up and takes a bite.*)

SCENE FIVE

WALLACE: "Broken Glass." By Wallace Kirkman. Age Thirteen. It's past four in the morning and I can't sleep. I go downstairs to get something to drink and maybe see what's on television. I open the refrigerator and take out the orange juice. I drink orange juice because I'm susceptible to colds. And because I heard that Coke rots your teeth. Whether it does or not makes no difference, because after you hear something like that, it stays in your brain. So I pour some orange juice into a glass and put the carton back in the fridge. And I drink. It goes down smooth and cold, and I just swallow it all without stopping. When I'm done, I look at the empty glass in my hand. My parents got a truckload of glassware for their wedding, and the glass in my hand is one of the set. It's older than me. Respect your elders, I think, but then I see her. She's laughing at me. She's inside the glass, laughing at me. I throw the glass against the refrigerator and hear it crash. I look at the shards on the floor. Like an invitation. I know that glass is made of sand, and I like walking on the beach, and I almost step toward the glass, but I don't. I think of blood. My blood. And I just kneel down and stare at the broken glass on the floor, watching for any reflection of the moonlight outside the kitchen window and waiting for my father to come downstairs, because he can't sleep through anything.

SCENE SIX

(Psychiatrist's office. PSYCHIATRIST *is sitting in a chair writing in a notebook.* WALLACE *walks in.)*

PSYCHIATRIST: You must be Wallace.

WALLACE: Yeah, I'm him.

PSYCHIATRIST: Pleased to meet you. Would you like to have a seat?

WALLACE: Can I lie on the couch?

PSYCHIATRIST: If you'd like.

WALLACE: It seems like the proper thing to do.

PSYCHIATRIST: Go right ahead.

WALLACE: I should *warn* you that I've had my head measured by a close friend, and if you shrink it by so much as a *millimeter,* I'm taking you to *court.*

PSYCHIATRIST: I don't shrink heads.

WALLACE: If I say "*I* do," does that make me insane?

PSYCHIATRIST: It's not that simple.

(WALLACE lies down on the couch.)

WALLACE: Nice couch. Where'd you get it?

PSYCHIATRIST: Bloomingdale's.

WALLACE: Really? I would have thought there'd be some store that would sell special couches for psychiatrists. It doesn't feel as good when you know that anybody with a few bucks can get one.

PSYCHIATRIST: Tell me why you're here, Wallace.

WALLACE: It was either this or a straitjacket, I suppose.

PSYCHIATRIST: Why's that?

WALLACE: Come on, didn't my father tell you all this?

PSYCHIATRIST: I'd like to hear what you have to say.

WALLACE: Can't argue with that. You see, I've been breaking glasses. In the kitchen.

PSYCHIATRIST: Any particular reason?

WALLACE: I like to live dangerously. You know, in perpetual fear of slicing the soles of my feet open. I don't know what it is, but ever since they cut the umbilical cord, I've been obsessed with *sharp* things. Especially knives. I'm attracted to knives. I'm *incredibly* attracted to *doctors* with knives. Do *you* have a knife, Doctor?

PSYCHIATRIST: No—

WALLACE: Do you want to *buy* one?

PSYCHIATRIST: No.

WALLACE: Oh.

(Long pause.)

PSYCHIATRIST: Tell me about your mother, Wallace.

WALLACE: She was like Sylvia Plath without the publishing contract.

PSYCHIATRIST: Do you remember much about her?

WALLACE: *Nothing.*

PSYCHIATRIST: Nothing at all?

WALLACE: Nope.

PSYCHIATRIST: Are you sure?

WALLACE: Why are you asking me this? Tell me, would you ask me this if my father weren't paying you?

PSYCHIATRIST: You're upset because your father made you come here.

WALLACE: No, I'm upset because he didn't pick a prettier psychiatrist.

PSYCHIATRIST: Was your *mother* pretty, Wallace?

WALLACE: *(Pause.)* Yeah, she was pretty. *Pretty* pretty. Pretty *suicidal.* And now she's pretty *dead.*

PSYCHIATRIST: You know, Wallace, you don't have to say anything you don't *want* to say.

WALLACE: Okay.

(Long silence.)

PSYCHIATRIST: What are you thinking about, Wallace? *(Pause.)* Wallace? *(Pause.)* Wallace?

SCENE SEVEN

The park. WALLACE *and* VICTORIA *walk in.* WALLACE *is eating a Mallo Cup and drinking something pink out of a bottle.* VICTORIA *is eating Jujyfruits.*

VICTORIA: Good movie.

WALLACE: Yeah.

VICTORIA: I like the kissing stuff.

WALLACE: I like when the girl died.

VICTORIA: You want to sit down here?

WALLACE: Here?

VICTORIA: Yeah. Sure.

WALLACE: Yeah. Sure.

(WALLACE *and* VICTORIA *sit down on a bench.*)

VICTORIA: You want a Jujyfruit?

WALLACE: No, they stick to your teeth. You want a Mallo Cup?

VICTORIA: Chocolate makes you break out.

WALLACE: Oh.

(WALLACE *takes a bite out of a Mallo Cup and drinks from his bottle.*)

VICTORIA: What is that?

WALLACE: What is *what*?

VICTORIA: *That.* In the bottle. The pink stuff.

WALLACE: Oh. You don't want to know.

VICTORIA: Sure I do. Wouldn't ask if I didn't want to know.

WALLACE: Uh, well, it's Pepto-Bismol mixed with seltzer.

VICTORIA: *What?*

WALLACE: I've got this perpetually upset stomach, and drinking this helps. It isn't all that bad, actually. Want some?

VICTORIA: No, thanks. I'll pass. *(Pause.)* It's such a nice day.

WALLACE: Yeah, it's not bad.

VICTORIA: I don't want to go back to school. Do you?

WALLACE: Oh, I'm just *dying* to sharpen my pencils and do tons of homework every night.

VICTORIA: Do you think eighth grade is going to be any different from seventh grade?

WALLACE: Nah, no chance. It's all the same. I don't think it matters. They just keep us in school until we're safely through our growth spurts and all of the puberty confusion, then send us out to make the best of the rest of our lives. And we get so terrified of the real world that we pay some university to keep us for four more years or eight more years or whatever. It all depends on how terrified you are. My grandmother's brother is sixty-two; he's *still* taking classes up in Chicago. If they keep you long enough to get comfortable when you're young, they've got you for *life*.

VICTORIA: Not me, that's for sure. Once I'm out, I'm *out*. I'm not going to college, no *way*.

WALLACE: What are you going to do?

VICTORIA: Who knows? Sit on the beach and get a really solid tan. Watch a lot of movies. Dance.

WALLACE: Sounds pretty stimulating, Victoria.

VICTORIA: Don't tease me.

WALLACE: I wasn't.

VICTORIA: Yes, you were.

WALLACE: I swear, I was not teasing you. Why would I tease you?

VICTORIA: I don't know. *(Pause.)* You didn't like the kissing stuff?

WALLACE: Huh?

VICTORIA: You know, in the movie.

WALLACE: Oh, I don't know.

VICTORIA: Sure you do.

WALLACE: I was getting candy. I missed it. Leave me alone.

VICTORIA: You want to try?

WALLACE: Try what?

VICTORIA: *That.*

WALLACE: What's *that?*

VICTORIA: Kissing.

WALLACE: You mean, with *you?*

VICTORIA: Yeah.

WALLACE: You mean, *now?*

VICTORIA: Yeah.

WALLACE: Umm—

VICTORIA: Scared?

WALLACE: Yeah, *right.* Go ahead. Kiss me.

VICTORIA: You sure?

WALLACE: As Shore as Dinah.

VICTORIA: *Dinah?*

WALLACE: Forget it. Will you kiss me already?

VICTORIA: Okay.

(VICTORIA *takes out the Jujyfruit she was eating and throws it away. They kiss.*)

WALLACE: You didn't fade out.

VICTORIA: Nope.

WALLACE: I think I love you, Victoria.

VICTORIA: Really?

(WALLACE *grabs* VICTORIA *and starts kissing her with great passion, holding her in his arms. After a few moments she breaks away.*)

WALLACE: What's wrong?

VICTORIA: What's *wrong?* You're too *fast* for me, Wallace, *that's* what's wrong. (VICTORIA *walks out.*)

WALLACE: Too *fast?* (Pause.) I mistook love for a girl who ate *Jujyfruits.* (WALLACE *drinks from his bottle.*)

SCENE EIGHT

Grandmother's kitchen. WALLACE *is sitting at the table.* GRANDMOTHER *walks in with a glass of milk and a plate of cookies.*

GRANDMOTHER: Tollhouse cookies, baked this morning especially for *you.*

WALLACE: Thanks.

GRANDMOTHER: You look wonderful. Such a *handsome* thing.

WALLACE: This is delicious.

GRANDMOTHER: Of *course* it is. Would I serve you anything *but?* The first batch went to Grandpa, so *terrible.* *(Pause.)* I'm so *happy* you came to visit.

WALLACE: I love to visit you guys.

GRANDMOTHER: That's like sugar on my heart. It makes me feel so good.

(WALLACE *points to a photograph in a frame on the table.*)

WALLACE: Who's this?

GRANDMOTHER: That's Grandpa's second cousin, Jerry. He just died. That's the last picture of him, taken *two minutes* before he went. He was at a wedding there, sitting at his table, in between two pretty young girls—you see? The photographer snapped this picture, Jerry was joking and flirting with these young girls—he was like that, Jerry, so *bad.* Two minutes later he just *shut his eyes.* *(Pause.)* Gone. But still smiling.

WALLACE: *(Pause.)* Nice picture. *(Pause.)* Grandma, can I ask you something stupid?

GRANDMOTHER: If it makes you happy, I don't see why *not.*

WALLACE: What was your first kiss like?

GRANDMOTHER: My first *kiss?* You really have faith in my memory, don't you?

WALLACE: You don't have to tell me.

GRANDMOTHER: No, no, no. Let's see. It was with Grandpa, and we were—

WALLACE: Your first kiss was with *Grandpa?*

GRANDMOTHER: Sure. We were steadies in *high* school, you know.

WALLACE: I just never really thought about it. *(Pause.)* Was it nice?

GRANDMOTHER: I was petrified, but he made me feel comfortable. Still petrified, but in a comfortable way. Comfortably petrified. It was on a Saturday night, in 1936, I think. We were in Wentworth Park, about four blocks from here.

WALLACE: Wow.

GRANDMOTHER: I remember thinking he kissed really wonderfully. I mean, we were just in high school, and kissing him made me feel like the movie stars must have felt. I almost fell *backward,* I was so taken away. Then I got suspicious, asking myself where'd he *learned* to kiss like that. When I asked him—

WALLACE: You *asked* him?

GRANDMOTHER: I *asked* him, and he told me he had been practicing on his pillow for almost five years. That made me feel better. Besides, with those eyes, I couldn't help but believe him. *(Pause.)* I was sixteen then. Generations are different.

WALLACE: Yeah.

GRANDMOTHER: Each generation changes. It either improves or declines.

WALLACE: Yeah, trouble is, you can't tell one from the other. I mean, what *your* generation calls decline, *mine* calls improvement. It's so confusing. Along with everything else.

GRANDMOTHER: Don't waste your time thinking of it. I will say one thing, though. Hair is important. Secondary, but important nonetheless. Find a girl with *hair*.

WALLACE: *Hair?*

GRANDMOTHER: Sure. I mean, I can't run my fingers through Grandpa's hair. All I can do is rub his scalp. *(Pause.)* Which some say brings good luck.

WALLACE: I think that's when you rub *Buddha's* scalp.

GRANDMOTHER: Well, Grandpa's certainly not *Buddha*. And I'm certainly not *lucky*.

WALLACE: *(Pause.)* Do you ever miss Mommy?

GRANDMOTHER: All the time.

WALLACE: *(Pause.)* Me, too. *(Pause.)* All the time.

GRANDMOTHER: *(Pause.)* Drink your milk. It's good for your teeth.

SCENE NINE

WALLACE: "My Mother's Turtlenecks." By Wallace Kirkman. Age Sixteen. My mother loved my father and hated her neck. She thought it was too fleshy or something. If I hated *my* neck, I'd have it removed, but my mother never trusted doctors, so she wore turtlenecks. All the time. In every picture we have of her, she's wearing a turtleneck. She had turtlenecks in every color of the rainbow. She had blacks, she had whites, she had grays, she had plaids, she had polka dots and hound's-tooth checks and stripes and Mickey Mouse and even a sort of *mesh* turtleneck. I can't picture her without a turtleneck on. Although, according to Freud, I *try* to, every moment of every day. We have a photograph of me when I was a baby wearing one of my mother's turtlenecks. *Swimming* in one of my mother's turtlenecks is more like it. Just a bald head and a big shirt. It's very erotic, in an Oedipal shirtwear sort of way. It's a rare photograph, because I'm smiling. I didn't smile all that much during most of my childhood. I'm taking lessons now, trying to learn again, but it takes time. I stopped smiling when my mother stopped wearing turtlenecks. I came home from a typical day in the second grade to find her taking a bath in her own blood on the kitchen floor. Her turtleneck was on top of the kitchen table, so it wouldn't come between her neck and her knife. I understood then why she had worn turtlenecks all along. To stop the blood from flowing. To cover the wound that was there all along. They tried to cover the wound when they buried her with one of her favorite turtleneck dresses on, but it didn't matter. It was just an empty hole by then. My mother wasn't hiding inside. *(Pause.)* She wrote a note before she died, asking to be cremated, and I asked my father why she wasn't. He said my mother was two women, and the one he loved would have been scared of the flames. *(Pause.)* I look at that photograph of little me inside my mother's shirt all the time. It's the closest I can get to security. There are no pictures of me inside mother's womb, but her turtleneck is close enough.

SCENE TEN

Wallace's bedroom. WALLACE *and* SARAH *are sitting on the bed.* SARAH *is reading something on a piece of paper.*

SARAH: Oh, I *really* like it.

WALLACE: *Really?*

SARAH: *Really.* It's very good.

WALLACE: *Why?*

SARAH: Well, it's funny, but it's also *sad.* It's really *sad.* And it's so *true.* I mean, there's so much of *you* in there. I mean, if I didn't know you, I'd *know* you after I read this. You know what I mean? I think it's really talented work. What's it for?

WALLACE: *For?*

SARAH: I mean, is it for English class or something?

WALLACE: No. I just sort of *wrote* it. Not really *for* anything. For me, I guess.

SARAH: You should submit it to the school newspaper. I bet they'd publish it.

WALLACE: I don't think I want the whole school reading this.

SARAH: Why not? I mean, you shouldn't be *ashamed* or anything—

WALLACE: I'm not *ashamed.* It just seems a little *sensationalist,* you know?

SARAH: I don't know. I guess so.

WALLACE: *So. (Pause.)* What do you want to do?

SARAH: Oh, I don't know.

WALLACE: We could go see a movie.

SARAH: Sure.

WALLACE: Or we could stay here.

SARAH: Sure.

WALLACE: Well, which one?

SARAH: Whichever.

WALLACE: Come on, I'm horrible with decisions.

SARAH: So am I.

WALLACE: Sarah, you're the valedictorian of our *class.* If you can't make a decision, who can?

SARAH: Umm, do you want to . . . stay *here?*

WALLACE: Yes.

SARAH: Okay. Let's stay here, then.

WALLACE: Settled. Do you want something to drink?

SARAH: Umm, sure.

WALLACE: What do you want? Some wine? A screwdriver?

SARAH: Oh, you mean something to *drink.* I don't drink.

WALLACE: Oh. *(Pause.)* Do you mind if I drink something?

SARAH: Oh, no, don't let me stand in your way.

WALLACE: I'll be right back.

SARAH: Okay.

(WALLACE *walks out.* SARAH *looks around the room. She looks at a photograph in a frame by the bed.* WALLACE *walks in, sipping a glass of wine.*)

WALLACE: *In vino veritas.*

SARAH: Who's this?

WALLACE: It's my mother.

SARAH: She was beautiful.

WALLACE: She was okay. I'm going to light a candle, okay?

SARAH: Sure.

(WALLACE *gets a candle. He takes a lighter from his pocket.*)

WALLACE: My great-grandfather was lighting a pipe with this lighter when he died. It's a Zippo. Pretty sharp, huh?

SARAH: It's very nice.

(WALLACE *tries to light the lighter. It won't light.*)

WALLACE: I think it has to warm up. *(Pause.* WALLACE *tries to light the lighter a few more times. It won't light.)* Uhh, I guess my great-grandfather forgot to *refill* it before he died. It's just as well. I hate candles. They're so *clichéd. (Pause.)* You want to listen to some music?

SARAH: Sure.

WALLACE: What do you like?

SARAH: Oh, *anything.*

WALLACE: You like James Taylor?

SARAH: Sure.

WALLACE: Let me just find the tape. (WALLACE *looks for the tape.*) I don't know where I put it. Maybe it's out in the car. I can go check—

SARAH: That's okay. We don't *need* music. Do we?

WALLACE: Uhh, *no,* I guess *not. (Pause.) Well.*

SARAH: What was your mother like, Wallace?

WALLACE: What was she *like?*

SARAH: Yeah.

WALLACE: She was like Sylvia Plath without a Fulbright scholarship.

SARAH: What do you mean?

WALLACE: I mean—I don't know what I mean, I'm *sixteen.* (WALLACE *drinks his glass of wine.*)

WALLACE: Would you mind if I kissed you?

SARAH: The wine works fast.

WALLACE: No, *I* do. Can I?

SARAH: Umm, can't we *talk* for a while?

WALLACE: I don't *want* to talk, I want to *kiss.* Can I kiss you?

SARAH: I'd really feel better if we just—

WALLACE: Oh, come *on.* (WALLACE *kisses* SARAH *long and hard.*)

SARAH: Maybe I should go.

WALLACE: What? Oh, come on—

SARAH: No, I mean, maybe this wasn't such a good idea.

WALLACE: Don't you *like* me?

SARAH: Very much, Wallace. But I don't want this to be just—I don't know, a lot of *stupidity*. Just kissing and nothing else. I wanted to *talk* to you, you know?

WALLACE: Yeah, whatever.

SARAH: Oh, Wallace, don't do that—

WALLACE: Just go, please.

SARAH: What?

WALLACE: You said maybe you should leave, so leave. I don't want to—I just don't want to *deal* with this, okay?

SARAH: But—

WALLACE: But *nothing*. Just, please, go, okay?

SARAH: I—*fine.* 'Bye, Wallace.

WALLACE: Yeah, yeah, *see* you—

SARAH: I'm sorry this didn't work out. *(Pause.)* I'll see you in school on Monday. Okay? *(Pause.)* Okay, 'bye.

(SARAH *walks out.*)

SCENE ELEVEN

Wallace's bedroom. WALLACE *is sitting on his bed, talking on the phone.*

WALLACE: Yeah, I wanted to see if I could make a song request and a dedication. . . . Umm, "Something in the Way She Moves" . . . by James Taylor. . . . You *don't?* I mean, it's on "Greatest Hits." You see, I'm trying to right a wrong, as they say. . . . I don't know, it's an expression. . . . Umm, do you have any, I don't know, like, Cat Stevens or something, somebody *close* to James Taylor? You know, one man and a guitar, that sort of thing. . . . Only top forty? . . . Who's *in* the top forty? Anybody named James? . . . No, that's not really appropriate. . . . Umm, could I just make a dedication, then? . . . Well, I *know* it's supposed to be for a song, but you don't seem to have the song I *need,* so if I could just maybe make the dedication and then you could maybe not play anything for about three minutes in *place* of the song I need and that way—hello? *(Pause.)* Wonderful. (WALLACE *hangs up the phone.)*

SCENE TWELVE

Sarah's front door. SARAH *inside,* WALLACE *outside.*

SARAH: Wallace.

WALLACE: Sarah.

SARAH: What are you doing here?

WALLACE: I wanted—umm, I wanted to *apologize.*

SARAH: You don't *have* to—

WALLACE: Yeah, I do.

SARAH: Okay. *(Pause.)* So?

WALLACE: You know, I just—it's funny, you know, sometimes I just wish I were a little kid again, when "sorry" was okay, you know?

SARAH: Yeah, well, we're not little kids, Wallace.

WALLACE: We're *not?* Umm, no, no, we're *not.* We're *certainly* not. Umm—*okay. Well.* I was acting *really* stupid before, I mean, just very—*stupid.* It was—I was being, umm—

SARAH: Stupid.

WALLACE: *Yeah.* And it was *wrong,* and it was—you know, it made you—it was *unfair.* And I *apologize.*

SARAH: Okay—

WALLACE: And I thought maybe we could try *again*.

SARAH: Again?

WALLACE: Yeah, you know, maybe I could come *in*—

SARAH: My parents are sleeping.

WALLACE: Oh. *(Pause.)* I could try to be quiet.

SARAH: It's kind of *late*.

WALLACE: Umm, well, you know, maybe you could come back over to my house and we could start from the *beginning*.

SARAH: *Wallace*—

WALLACE: I mean, I know it *sounds* like a stupid idea, but trust me, I'll behave this time, I know what to do. We can *talk*. We can have a *conversation*. We don't even have to kiss, we'll just *talk* and then you can go. *(Pause.)* Or we can just sit in *silence* for a while. We don't *have* to talk.

SARAH: I don't think that's a very good *idea*, Wallace.

WALLACE: All I'm *asking* for is another chance, Sarah. Don't make me beg.

SARAH: There's no need to *beg*, Wallace, I just don't think—

WALLACE: Okay. I'll beg. (WALLACE *drops to his knees.*)

WALLACE: I'm *begging*, Sarah, give me another shot.

SARAH: Wallace—

WALLACE: I'll be *good*.

SARAH: *Wallace*—

WALLACE: Look at the moon, Sarah. It's *full*. It's *romantic*.

SARAH: Wallace, get off your knees.

WALLACE: *(Pause.)* That's okay. I kind of like it down here. *In the heartland.*

SARAH: What?

WALLACE: Nothing. *(Pause.)* I was going to bring a guitar and maybe *serenade* you, but I can't sing. And I don't play the guitar. I did have Romantic Thoughts, though.

SARAH: That's very sweet, Wallace. *(Pause.)* I really should go back *inside*—

WALLACE: Yeah, I understand. You know, I tried to dedicate a song to you on the radio, you know, something by James Taylor, and they didn't *have* any James Taylor. Can you *believe* that?

SARAH: That's pretty funny.

WALLACE: Yeah. Pretty funny world.

SARAH: Sure is.

WALLACE: So, umm, you wouldn't want to maybe try again, say, *next* weekend? A movie or—

SARAH: *Wallace.*

WALLACE: No, I understand. Okay.

SARAH: I'm *sorry,* Wallace.

WALLACE: Yeah, no, *I'm* sorry.

SARAH: *(Pause.)* Are you going to *stay* down there?

WALLACE: For a little while, yeah. If you don't mind.

SARAH: No, I don't mind.

WALLACE: Thanks.

SARAH: Yeah, well, okay. Good night, Wallace.

WALLACE: 'Night.

SARAH: 'Bye.

WALLACE: 'Bye.

(SARAH *walks out, closing the door behind her. Pause.* WALLACE *looks up at the moon.*)

WALLACE: Thanks a lot, Moon. You really came through for me.

SCENE THIRTEEN

Psychiatrist's office. PSYCHIATRIST *is sitting in a chair, writing in a notebook.* WALLACE *walks in.*

PSYCHIATRIST: Hello, Wallace. It's been a long time since I've seen you.

WALLACE: About five years.

PSYCHIATRIST: Yes. Nice to see you again.

WALLACE: I'll bet.

PSYCHIATRIST: Would you like to have a seat?

WALLACE: No.

PSYCHIATRIST: Okay, then. What's on your mind?

WALLACE: Lots. *(Pause.)* I came here last time because my father made me, but now I'm here because I want to talk to you. You see, I'm confused. My mother makes me a sandwich for lunch. I take it. She, in turn, slits her throat. And after the funeral, when I go back to school for the first time, my *father* makes me a sandwich for lunch, or at least he *tries,* so as not to screw up my daily routine any more than it already has been. And I'm thinking, all day while I'm in school, that *he's* going to be lying on the kitchen floor when I get home. It's the same thing, you see, because I *took* the sandwich. If I didn't *take,* I think, they'll be okay. But I *take,* and that kills them. And when I came home from school and he *wasn't* on the floor of the kitchen, but instead sitting in his study, *alive,* I was disappointed. Let down. Because my system didn't work. It *failed* me. Everything was *failing* me. And when I *expected* my father to fail me, he failed me by *not* failing me. He was just sitting there in his study. Alone, deserted by the woman he loved and planned to —I don't know, move to Florida with, and he can manage to stay alive, to go on living. *How?* And, I mean, Victoria, this thirteen-year-old *girl,* is *sitting* there, practically *begging* me to kiss her, I mean, she would have been on her *knees* in a second, in more ways than one, that's how it seemed, and when I finally let down and actually *do* what she's been *asking* me to do—I *kiss* her and *bang*—all of a sudden, *I'm* too *fast* for her. I told her I *loved* her, and she runs off, *skipping,* and the next week she's kissing somebody else, and I heard he got up her *shirt,* and *he's* not too fast, *I'm* the one who was too *fast.* So I get this reputation that completely *terrifies* me, because, not only will no *decent* girls *look* at me, I can't even think about any of the *in*decent girls, because I'm scared to death of having to live up to my own reputation. And, now, I mean, when my big mistake has always been talking too much, so I try, finally, on this girl I *really* like, okay, I mean, *bright, pretty,* actually *nice, caring,* I try not to screw it up by talking too much, and I go *right* for the kiss, and she won't ever see me again because I didn't talk too much. I mean, I can't *win.* They *desert.* Women *desert.* And I know it all stems back to my lousy *coward* mother, and if she hadn't *offed* herself, I'd have no problems, but what I'm trying to say is I don't know what to *do* about all of this, Doctor, and it's my life, so can—you know, can you give me some *advice* or something, Doctor? *(Pause.)* Doctor? *(Pause.)* Doctor?

SCENE FOURTEEN

WALLACE *and* PSYCHIATRIST.

WALLACE: "Tyrannosaurus Rex." By Wallace Kirkman. Age Eighteen.

(PSYCHIATRIST *gets up and starts to walk out.*)

WALLACE: Don't go. I need *help* with this one. Stay right there. Please. You'll like this. It's very *Freudian*. In fact, it's a *dream*.

(*The lights change rather dramatically.* PSYCHIATRIST *sits, and* WALLACE *walks out. He walks in a moment later with a crate of props.*)

WALLACE: I need a *mother. (Pause.)* I need somebody who can *act* like a mother.

(VICTORIA *walks in.*)

WALLACE: You'll do. I always wanted to be a dinosaur when I was young. Young*er*. I have a lot in common with Tyrannosaurus. We both walk on two legs, we both eat meat, and we both occasionally answer to the nickname "King of the Tyrant Lizards." Anyhow, the recipe for this dream is something like two parts *Oedipus Rex*, two parts Freud, and nineteen parts me. In the beginning, the eventual parents are both thirteen years old.

(WALLACE *pushes* PSYCHIATRIST *and* VICTORIA *onto their knees.*)

WALLACE: And Jewish.

(WALLACE *pulls two pairs of gag glasses out of the crate of props. He puts one—with a plastic nose—on* VICTORIA *and the other—with a plastic nose and a plastic mustache—on* PSYCHIATRIST.)

WALLACE: They get bar mitzvahed and bat mitzvahed on the same day and sleep with each other on the same night. Kids today. God bless 'em. On with the dream. The girl gets pregnant, as girls will do.

(WALLACE *pulls a baby doll out of the crate of props and hands it to* VICTORIA.)

WALLACE: She wants to get an abortion so the baby won't get in the way of the seventh grade, but neither of the partners got any cash for their *mitzvahs,* only savings bonds. *Lots* of savings bonds. So, they pack several pairs of underwear and go to stay with the girl's grandmother, a mentally ill fortune-teller from Boston.

(GRANDMOTHER *walks in—a grand entrance—wearing a turban.*)

GRANDMOTHER: This baby is *trouble.* He's going to fight with you and *shtoop* you.

VICTORIA: *Shtoop?*

PSYCHIATRIST: How do you know the baby's going to be a "he"?

GRANDMOTHER: I'm a fortune-teller. Give me a break.

WALLACE: When the baby is born, they immediately sell it on the black market.

(VICTORIA *tosses the baby doll to* WALLACE. WALLACE *pulls a packet of play money out of the crate of props and hands it to* VICTORIA.)

WALLACE: They use the money to pay a few months' worth of rent on a Beacon Street apartment.

(WALLACE *takes the packet of play money from* VICTORIA *and replaces it in the crate of props. He pulls a pair of boxing gloves out of the crate of props and hands them to* PSYCHIATRIST, *who puts them on.*)

WALLACE: The father starts taking boxing lessons. The mother spends her spare time in their spare apartment reading spare Japanese literature.

(WALLACE *pulls a Mishima paperback out of the crate of props and tosses it to* VICTORIA.)

WALLACE: They earn rent money and grocery money and boxing-lesson money and Japanese-book money by becoming kiddie porn stars.

(PSYCHIATRIST *and* VICTORIA *look at one another in* horror.*)*

WALLACE: *Cut.* And, at this point, the dream leaps ahead about seventeen years or so. The father is a very popular amateur boxer.

(WALLACE *pulls* PSYCHIATRIST *up off her knees so that she is standing.* WALLACE *pulls* VICTORIA *up off her knees so that she is also standing.)*

WALLACE: The mother is about to commit ritual suicide.

(WALLACE *pulls the large knife* MOTHER *used to slit her throat out of the crate of props and hands it to* VICTORIA.)

VICTORIA: I've tried and tried and *tried.* And I'll just *never* be Japanese.

(VICTORIA *plunges the large knife into her bowels and falls to the floor. Dead.* WALLACE *stares at her for a moment, then tosses the baby doll into the crate of props and pulls out a pair of boxing gloves. He puts them on.)*

WALLACE: The son is a boxing necrophiliac who masturbates. A lot.

(WALLACE *approaches* GRANDMOTHER.)

WALLACE: Hello.

GRANDMOTHER: *Shalom.*

WALLACE *(to the audience):* I *hate* when people say, "Shalom." I never know whether they're *coming* or *going* or just a *pacifist.*

GRANDMOTHER: How may I serve you?

WALLACE: I'd like to know my fortune.

GRANDMOTHER: Easy. You're going to fight with your dad and *shtoop* your mom. Ten bucks, please.

WALLACE: This is *horrible.* I don't want to fight with Dad. I *love* Dad.

GRANDMOTHER: Ten bucks, please.

WALLACE: And I don't want to *shtoop* Mom. Because Dad would get mad. And we'd fight.

GRANDMOTHER: Ten bucks, please.

WALLACE: And I don't want to fight with Dad. I *love* Dad. Boy, this makes me tense. I need some *release.*

GRANDMOTHER: Ten bucks, please.

(WALLACE *punches* GRANDMOTHER *and knocks her out.)*

WALLACE: I wonder if there's anything good over at the *morgue.*

(WALLACE *looks at* VICTORIA.)

WALLACE: She's *beautiful.* She's *everything.* She's *dead. And* she's a nice Jewish girl. I wonder where her bowels are.

(WALLACE *leaps onto* VICTORIA, *kisses her madly for a few moments, then rolls off onto the floor.)*

WALLACE: It's time to *box.*

(WALLACE *approaches* PSYCHIATRIST.)

WALLACE: You want to fight?

PSYCHIATRIST: Sure.

(A bell rings. PSYCHIATRIST *punches* WALLACE *and knocks him out.)*

PSYCHIATRIST: Ten, nine, eight, seven, six, five, four, three, two, one.

*(*PSYCHIATRIST *slaps* WALLACE's *face and he comes to.)*

WALLACE: Did I win?

PSYCHIATRIST: Nope.

WALLACE: Boo.

PSYCHIATRIST: Come on, I'll buy you a beer.

WALLACE: I'm underage.

PSYCHIATRIST: You don't have a fake ID?

WALLACE: I was always too busy *masturbating* to buy one.

PSYCHIATRIST: Oh. *(Pause.)* Come on, I'll buy you a ginger ale.

WALLACE: Yeah, okay. You're on.

*(*PSYCHIATRIST *helps* WALLACE *up, and they walk a few steps.)*

PSYCHIATRIST: One beer and one ginger ale, barkeep.

WALLACE: Excuse me for a moment, I've got to go to the bathroom.

PSYCHIATRIST: But you haven't had anything to drink.

WALLACE: *(Pause.) Excuse me for a moment, I've got to go to the bathroom.*

PSYCHIATRIST: Oh. Sure, go right ahead.

WALLACE: Be right back.

(WALLACE *walks out. He runs in a few moments later, without the boxing gloves on, his hands covering his eyes. He is* screaming. GRANDMOTHER, PSYCHIATRIST, *and* VICTORIA *clear the stage and walk out. The lights change back.* WALLACE *takes his hands off his tightly closed eyes, opens them, sees nobody around, and stops screaming. He yawns, as if waking up.*)

WALLACE: I've been having this dream every night for the past two months. It's always pretty much the same, although sometimes it's in color and sometimes it's in black and white, and once the black-and-white version was colorized, which pissed me off. I mean, it's more or less my life story, and who wants their life story *colorized?*

SCENE FIFTEEN

Wallace's dormitory room. WALLACE *and* LILI *walk in.*

WALLACE: This is my room.

LILI: Nice. How did you get a single room your first year?

WALLACE: I had a psychiatrist write the school a note saying essentially that if I had to live with another person, I'd probably kill them.

LILI: Seriously?

WALLACE: Not really. But the school believed it. *(Pause.)* You must be tired.

LILI: Why?

WALLACE: Well, I mean, you were onstage for practically the entire time.

LILI: It's an important part.

WALLACE: And you did it so well. *Really.* The whole thing was— *beautiful.*

LILI: The choreographer's pretty talented.

WALLACE: I mean, who would ever think to do *Catcher in the Rye* as a *ballet?*

LILI: The *choreographer* would.

WALLACE: I—well, I mean, I *know,* but it's just—*wow.* You know, I never realized there was so much stuff about *lesbians* in *Catcher in the Rye.*

LILI: It's all in the *subtext.*

WALLACE: Yeah. But I think, you know, having *you*—you know, having a *woman* as Holden Caulfield really made everything *quite* clear.

LILI: I'm glad you liked it. *(Pause.)* You're very *cute,* Wallace.

WALLACE: *Me?*

LILI: Yes, you. I'm really *drawn* to you, you know?

WALLACE: Umm, *sure.*

LILI: What are you waiting for?

WALLACE: Huh?

LILI: *Kiss* me.

WALLACE: Umm, are you—umm, *sure.*

(WALLACE *kisses* LILI.)

WALLACE: How was that?

LILI: That was nice. Do you want to sleep together?

WALLACE: *What?*

LILI: Do you want to *make love?*

WALLACE: Umm, with *you?*

LILI: *Yes,* with *me.*

WALLACE: Umm, sure, yes, yeah, *sure. (Pause.)* What do we do?

LILI: Are you a *virgin?*

WALLACE: Umm, *technically,* no.

LILI: What do you mean, "technically"?

WALLACE: Well, what is the definition of male virginity?

LILI: Is that a rhetorical question?

WALLACE: A male virgin is a male who has never had his thing inside a female's thing. Right?

LILI: Anybody still calling it a "thing" is probably a virgin, I know that much.

WALLACE: Well, when I was born, I had a thing. A very tiny, bald thing, but a thing nonetheless. And I entered this world through my mother's thing—the infamous "tunnel of love." Therefore, my thing has been inside of a female's thing, although it had to share the space with the rest of my body. In fact, pretty much all men are born nonvirgins. The only exceptions would be men born cesarean style.

LILI: You're saying you lost your virginity—with your *mother?*

WALLACE: Yeah.

LILI: You're pretty weird, Wallace.

WALLACE: Thank you.

LILI: So, will this be your first time having sex with somebody outside your immediate family?

WALLACE: You've got me there. Yes.

LILI: I'm *honored.*

WALLACE: I'm *terrified.*

LILI: It's simple. Don't worry, you'll be fine. Before we get started, do you have any protection?

WALLACE: Umm, no.

LILI: Here, take this.

(LILI *hands* WALLACE *a condom.*)

WALLACE: You really come prepared.

LILI: I don't want to even joke *around* with AIDS, you know?

WALLACE: I know. Remember when Ayds was just a dietetic candy? There's a stock that must have done *real* well. Can you picture the president of the company right before the end? "Call the thing Dexatrim, it's a *superb* name for a disease!"

LILI: You don't have to make jokes, Wallace, everything's going to be fine. *Better* than fine.

WALLACE: How did you know I was nervous? I thought I was covering it pretty well.

LILI: A woman knows.

WALLACE: Hey, tell me something.

LILI: Yeah?

WALLACE: What can you possibly see in me?

LILI: What do you mean?

WALLACE: I mean, how did I end up here with *you?* You're a beautiful senior, I'm a nervous little freshman.

LILI: You've got great eyes.

WALLACE: I *do?*

LILI: Really intelligent eyes. Like they've seen a *lot,* that's what they look like.

WALLACE: You're here with me because of my *eyes?*

LILI: Yeah, sort of.

WALLACE: The brochures don't do college justice.

LILI: Let's get on the *bed,* Wallace.

WALLACE: Let me just hit the lights.

LILI: No, keep them *on,* I want to *see* you.

WALLACE: You keep the lights on with a guy named Biff who pumps iron and gasoline. With a Jew from Jersey, you do it in the dark.

(WALLACE *flips the light switch. Blackout.)*

LILI: *(Pause.)* Why do you wear so many *layers?*

WALLACE: Wearing layers of clothing keeps you warmer than wearing one *thick* garment.

LILI: But it's not cold out.

WALLACE: All right, so I hate my body. I'm too skinny. Is that such a crime?

LILI: You've got a nice body.

WALLACE: In the *dark,* maybe. You're so *sweaty—*

LILI: I want to *see* you, Wallace, I want to see *all* of you. Can't you turn the lights on?

WALLACE: If the lights go on, I go in the closet.

LILI: Do you have a candle or something, at least?

WALLACE: I *hate* candles. *(Pause.)* Am I doing okay?

LILI: You're doing *fine*. Just *fine*.

WALLACE: *(Pause.)* Why did the chicken cross the road?

LILI: This isn't the *time*, Wallace.

WALLACE: Sorry.

(Long pause. WALLACE *flips the light switch. The lights come up. They sit up in bed together.)*

WALLACE: *Wow. (Pause.)* You know, I always wondered what this would be like, I always tried to imagine, and it's just—now it's *actual*. Now it's *real*. Now—I just slept with an older woman. An older woman who *dances*. Billy Corkscraw would never believe it.

LILI: *Who?*

WALLACE: This kid I was friends with growing up, Billy Corkscraw. He talked about sex all the time. He told me everything, little Mister Know-It-All. You know, told me that the only way to *really* satisfy a woman was to put Spanish fly in her drink, and if you were dating a girl who spoke French instead of Spanish, you had to get your Spanish fly "translated," which Billy said could only be done at the French embassy and it cost a lot of money, and he said we would probably just be better off paying professionals. *(Pause.)* He moved to Arizona when we were eleven. Last I heard about him, he couldn't find a date for his senior prom.

LILI: *(Pause.)* You have to meet my little *sister*.

SCENE SIXTEEN

Wallace's dormitory room. WALLACE *and* NINA *are sitting on the bed. She is looking at a photograph in a frame by the bed.*

NINA: Is this your mother?

WALLACE: Yeah. She's dead.

NINA: Oh. I'm sorry.

WALLACE: For what?

NINA: For asking.

WALLACE: I don't mind. I mean, I've lived without her for so long —it's not all that bad, really.

NINA: What was she like?

WALLACE: Like Sylvia Plath without talent.

NINA: She killed herself?

WALLACE: Yeah. When I was six.

NINA: That's too bad. How'd she kill herself?

WALLACE: You really want to know?

NINA: Yeah. If you don't want to talk about it, though—

WALLACE: No, I do. It's just that it freaks most people out. *(Pause.)* She slit her throat with a kitchen knife.

NINA: Oh, God. I never understand why people don't just take pills and die painlessly.

WALLACE: I guess if you hate yourself enough to want to die—it's just like if you wanted to kill someone else. If you hate something, you want it to die painfully. I mean, I guess that's what it is. I know that pain belongs in there somewhere.

NINA: How did you deal with all that? I mean, how'd you get through it?

WALLACE: I used to break glass.

NINA: Huh?

WALLACE: I used to break glasses on the kitchen floor. That helped a little. It was destructive, but it eased the pain.

NINA: How *sad*—

WALLACE: It's no big deal. I mean, I guess it made me who I am today, and who knows what I would have been if she was still alive. Maybe I'd be somebody I'd hate, you know. Sure, there are times I'd kill to have her back, just for a day. So I could show her something I've written, or talk to her about my thoughts, or just even to see her smile when I did something silly.

(Long pause.)

NINA: What are you thinking about?

WALLACE: I don't know. About my mother, and about how you listen to me talk, and—and about how I'd love to kiss you right now.

NINA: So why *don't* you?

WALLACE: What? Well, umm, Nina, do you—did your sister tell you—

NINA: I know. You and my sister were—*together.*

WALLACE: And it doesn't *bother* you?

NINA: A little. Not much. I mean, you were *drunk*—

WALLACE: *What?*

NINA: And all you did was *kiss*, right?

WALLACE: Umm—umm, *yeah.* Just a few drunken kisses, that's all it was.

NINA: A *few?* She said *one.*

WALLACE: Well, I mean, there were a few *within* the one. But we never pulled our lips apart, so technically, I guess, yeah, just *one.*

NINA: Okay. *(Pause.)* Well?

WALLACE: Well what?

NINA: *Kiss* me.

WALLACE: Nina, I think I *lóve* you. I know it sounds stupid, but— is that okay?

NINA: Sure.

WALLACE: Okay. I'm going to kiss you now, okay?

NINA: Okay.

WALLACE: Okay.

(They kiss.)

SCENE SEVENTEEN

Wallace's dormitory room. WALLACE *and* WENDY *are sitting on the bed, kissing.*

WENDY: Are you sure we should be doing this?

WALLACE: Why not?

WENDY: Well, what about your girlfriend?

WALLACE: What *about* her?

WENDY: Well—

WALLACE: I'm drunk, you're drunk, we don't know what we're doing. Right?

WENDY: Umm, *right.*

WALLACE: *Right.* Give me a kiss.

(They kiss.)

SCENE EIGHTEEN

WALLACE *in a spotlight.*

WALLACE: I did it. Mommy. I fell in love—*really*—for the first time. I mean, it wasn't romance for the sake of romance. It was romance for the sake of—*somebody. Nina.* Nina listened. And I got scared. I ran away. To somebody else. What do I do? Mommy. It *hurts. (Pause.)* I want my—I *need* my mother. *(Pause.)* I'm not asking for much. I just—all I want is to take the knife away from her. To go back and take the knife away from her. All I want to do is change history.

(The lights come up on the kitchen. MOTHER *is fixing a peanut butter and banana sandwich. She is peeling the banana.* WALLACE *looks at her. He looks at the audience, then looks back at her. He walks past the table, picking up the large knife as he goes by. He walks out.* MOTHER *finishes peeling the banana and fixes the sandwich, breaking the banana up with her hands and spreading the peanut butter with a spoon. She puts the sandwich into a lunchbox on the table.* WALLACE *runs in.)*

WALLACE: I'm going to miss the bus! Is my lunch ready?

MOTHER: All set.

(WALLACE grabs the lunchbox and kisses MOTHER *on the cheek.)*

WALLACE: 'Bye, Mommy.

MOTHER: 'Bye, Wallace.

WALLACE *(to the audience):* I love the second grade!

MOTHER: Don't shout, Wallace.

(WALLACE *runs out.* MOTHER *watches after him. She writes a note on a slip of paper. While she is writing the note,* WALLACE *walks in and quietly watches her from the side. She puts the note on the table. She takes off her turtleneck shirt, so she is in her brassiere. She wraps the turtleneck around her neck and pulls it taut, attempting to strangle herself. The lights on the kitchen slowly fade, and* WALLACE *is in the spotlight again.*)

WALLACE *(to the audience): (Pause.)* In countless science fiction stories about time travel, the moral is quite clear. When you go back in time, if you so much as step on an ant, the course of history will change drastically. Don't try to change history. It's dangerous. *(Pause.)* In my experience, trying to change history isn't really dangerous. It's just a waste of time—a futile, frustrating exercise where you exert yourself and use up boundless energies and—and everything stays exactly the same. With small technical differences, perhaps. One more dead ant. If you take a razor away from a man who wants to kill himself, he'll *still* kill himself—he just won't be clean shaven. The will is all that matters. If the will is there— *(Pause.)* I should dwell on the future. Dwelling on the past is hopeless.

SCENE NINETEEN

Wallace's dormitory room. WALLACE *is standing. There is a knock on the door.*

WALLACE: Yeah.

(NINA *walks in.*)

NINA: Hey, there.

WALLACE: Sit down.

NINA: What's wrong?

WALLACE: Sit down.

NINA: Okay.

(NINA *sits on the bed.*)

NINA: What's the matter?

WALLACE: You deserve better.

NINA: Huh?

WALLACE: I'm not good enough for you.

NINA: What are you talking about? You're the *best*.

WALLACE: I'm the *worst*. You should *hate* me.

NINA: Why?

WALLACE: You don't want to know.

NINA: *What* don't I want to know?

WALLACE: I've been with somebody else.

NINA: *(Pause.)* What?

WALLACE: I was with somebody else.

NINA: *(Pause.)* Who?

WALLACE: Wendy.

NINA: Wendy. *(Pause.)* I think I'm going to be sick.

(NINA *runs out.*)

WALLACE: *Nina. (Pause.)* Women *desert.*

(WALLACE *picks up a glass. He holds it in his hand, looking at it. He starts to throw it so that it will break against the wall.* NINA *walks in.*)

NINA: Don't you dare break that glass or I'll turn right around and I won't come back.

(WALLACE *stops. He puts the glass on the bed and looks at* NINA.)

WALLACE: You came back. *(Pause.)* You should hate me.

NINA: I do. But I also happen to love you, and I'm not going to lose you without a fight.

WALLACE: You came back.

NINA: Do you want to work through this? I'll tell you right now, it's not going to be easy.

WALLACE: I know.

NINA: You betrayed me.

WALLACE: I know.

NINA: I know you may have been scared or whatever, but I swear to God, if you ever do this again, both you and her—*whoever* she is —will be lying on the street, okay?

WALLACE: Okay. *(Pause.)* You came back.

NINA: You want to work through this?

WALLACE: Yes.

NINA: Okay. Then we will.

WALLACE: You came back.

(WALLACE *goes to hug* NINA. *They hug. After a few moments she breaks from the hug and slaps him, hard, across the face.)*

NINA: Don't you *ever* do that to me again, understand?

WALLACE: You came back.

SCENE TWENTY

Grandmother's kitchen. WALLACE *and* GRANDMOTHER *are sitting at the table.*

GRANDMOTHER: And you *really* love her?

WALLACE: I *swear.* At least, I think I do. I mean, I know I do. And I was running away from her. You know, I was so terrified that she'd leave me, I wanted to leave first so I wouldn't have to deal with the pain. You know, I *wanted* to get caught with this other girl, Grandma, I *had* to tell her about it right away. It all made sense when I told her. Too much sense. She said she was going to be sick and walked out of my room. And something in me clicked. Something in me had been expecting it. Had been expecting her to leave me. And it made sense. And it was complete. *(Pause.)* And then she came *back.* That's what threw me for a loop. And right then I said, There is no way I am going to lose her. I am going to do everything in my power to keep her. Because she came *back.* And it terrifies me that I almost lost her because Mommy killed herself. I mean, my mother deserts me for whatever reasons, but she almost made me lose the one girl I've ever really *loved.*

GRANDMOTHER: *(Pause.)* You can't *blame* her until you die, you know.

WALLACE: What?

GRANDMOTHER: Your mother. I mean, sure, you can invoke her name once in a while to clear up a messy situation, but you've got to be responsible for *something* eventually. A dead mother does not give you *carte blanche* for a lifetime of screwing up. You can *do* it —you can screw *up,* go right ahead, but don't keep blaming her, or you'll just go through life fooling yourself and you'll die a blind man. *(Pause.)* Understand?

WALLACE: I think so. I'm not sure.

GRANDMOTHER: It's okay. You're still young. *(Pause.)* Are they feeding you enough up at school? You look thin.

WALLACE: They're feeding me fine, Grandma.

(Pause. WALLACE points to a photograph in a frame on the table.)

WALLACE: Who's this?

GRANDMOTHER: Oh, that's Gertrude Mawsbaum, we grew up together. She just passed on. This picture was taken three weeks before she died.

EPILOGUE

WALLACE *is standing to the left with a tomato in his hand and a crate of tomatoes at his feet.* NINA *is standing to the right, wearing a white dress. Pause.*

NINA: Well?

WALLACE: *(Pause.)* I don't want to ruin your dress. *(Pause.)* I don't want to ruin your beautiful dress.

(Pause. The lights slowly fade.)

JONATHAN MARC SHERMAN

I was born in Morristown, New Jersey, and grew up in Livingston, New Jersey. I dropped out of Livingston High School in my senior year and now attend Bennington College. I started writing plays when I got a typewriter for my twelfth or thirteenth birthday, I don't remember which. My last play, *Serendipity and Serenity,* was given a staged reading in the Sixth Annual Young Playwrights Festival, and *Women and Wallace* was fully produced in the Seventh Annual Young Playwrights Festival. It's tough to communicate exactly what I got out of the experience. I met some interesting people and saw my words brought to life. The preliminary reading of the play, in May 1988, directed by James Lapine, with Robert Leonard as Wallace, was enormously helpful to me and remains a treasured memory. The production of the play in September and October 1988, directed by Don Scardino, with Josh Hamilton as Wallace, was more than I could have ever hoped for. The first time I heard the play draw out wonderful laughter from the audience. The shock I had while doing a rewrite when I realized I was writing Wallace with Josh's voice in my head and not my own. The blast of energy unleashed by a group of six young men at Show World Center the night the play finished its run at Playwrights Horizons. These are a few of the strange, inexplicable but meaningful memories I have. I won't know if I've learned all that much until the next one, which is coming up right behind you. Watch out.